WHO PROFITS

WHO
PROFITS

Winners, Losers, and
Government Regulation

ROBERT A. LEONE

Basic Books, Inc., Publishers   *New York*

Library of Congress Cataloging-in-Publication Data

Leone, Robert A.
  Who profits.

  Includes index.
    1. Trade regulation—United States. 2. Business and
politics—United States. 3. Costs, Industrial—United
States. I. Title.
HD3616.U47L44   1986   338.973   85–47992
ISBN   0–465–09183–0

To Mary, Andrea, and Elisa

Contents

PART II

UNDERSTANDING GOVERNMENT WHEN

COMPETITION MATTERS

Acknowledgments

No book is the work of a single writing assignment or a single author and this is no exception. For the past fifteen years I have worked on dozens of research and teaching assignments related to the impact of government on business, and this book is my effort to bring together what I have learned and observed from these efforts. Much of the research cited in this book is either the work of others or the product of efforts requiring the collaboration of valued colleagues. Accordingly, the ideas presented in this volume are necessarily the products of many individuals working together to address complicated problems. While I am more than happy to credit my colleagues with the quality of their ideas, I am not prepared to attribute to them any inaccuracies in my interpretation or ambiguities in my presentation of their contributions to this volume.

I would especially like to acknowledge John R. Meyer of the John F. Kennedy School of Government at Harvard for his intellectual stimulus to this enterprise. Twenty years ago Professor Meyer helped me disentangle the microeconomics of an economic problem involving the United States maritime industry, and ever since he has been a reliable source of creative perspectives and thoughtful criticisms. John is a valued colleague and friend, and I can only hope this project justifies the enthusiasm and support he has provided over the years.

I would also like to express my thanks to the late William Abernathy of the Graduate School of Business Administration at Harvard. Professor Abernathy was an important source of ideas on issues involving corporate strategy and the role government can play in influencing strategy. I never cease to be impressed by his insights on these matters, especially since his work is not usually identified with strategic management but with technological change in the manufacturing sector. Prior to his death, Bill and I had many hours of conversation on the concept of strategy. I hope that I have captured some of those ideas here in a useful way.

Still a third source of intellectual stimulus is Professor Mark Moore of the Kennedy School. While Mark and I have not done any collaborative work on matters of business/government relations, I cannot fail to acknowledge his intellectual contributions to this volume. Mark is responsible for the public management curriculum at the Kennedy School and has been my tutor on matters of strategic management in the public sector. He has helped me develop an appreciation of institutional issues I previously did not possess but now consider central to my conception of the nature of the business/government relationship.

I cite these three individuals because this book represents my effort to bring together the principles of applied microeconomics, corporate strategic thinking, and political analysis, and these are the three individuals who introduced me to the richness of these subject areas. Throughout this book, I have attempted to address no issue as solely an economic, strategic, or institutional issue. I have tried always to keep all three perspectives in view.

Intellectual stimulus without institutional support is not enough to get a book written. Thus I would like to acknowledge the support of the John F. Kennedy School of Government. Dean Graham Allison encouraged me to undertake this particular enterprise when I joined the School's faculty in 1981. More important, however, starting in 1977 the Kennedy School gave me the opportunity to teach in its midcareer program. Up to that time I had been teaching MBA and executive classes at the Harvard Business School exclusively. The opportunity to share my ideas with practicing government officials greatly enriched my research perspective. Indeed, it was the success of these initial efforts that led me to believe that it was possible to develop an analytical paradigm that would satisfy the needs of both private- and public-sector audiences.

Two of the Kennedy School's research centers have played an important role in the development of this book. The Center for Energy and Environmental Policy has supported much of my empirical research on business/government issues; hence the disproportionate number of energy and environmental examples in this volume. Professor William Hogan, the Center's director, has always supported my efforts enthusiastically. When at a critical juncture in the preparation of this volume I needed relief from my teaching obligations to the Center, Bill was unhesitating in his favorable response.

The Kennedy School's Center for Business and Government has also provided research support for this project. More important, however, Professor Winthrop Knowlton, the Center's director, has provided both thoughtful criticism and continuing encouragement. He helped me test many of the ideas on our students in the spring of 1985 in a collaborative teaching assignment. Both Win and the class displayed sufficient tolerance to justify my forging ahead.

Dean Hale Champion has also encouraged me to air these subjects with the Senior Executive Fellows at the School. These career senior governmental officials have done their best to keep this enterprise targeted on real-world challenges.

Just as I wish to acknowledge the support of my public-sector students, I would also like to acknowledge those with a largely private-sector perspective. In particular, those Harvard MBAs who chanced upon a course entitled "Government Regulation and Operating Policy" will recognize much of what they read here.

That course, by the way, had the odd title it did because Professor Meyer and I wanted a title with an appropriate bureaucratic acronym, since our colleagues had, unwittingly or otherwise, chosen course names with such acronyms. For example, a then popular course at the Kennedy School was entitled "Regulation of Business" or ROB. Some cynical people thought that ROB was what business regulation was all about. At the same time there was a course at the Business School entitled "Managing in a Regulated Environment" or MIRE. Again, there were many people who felt that MIRE was an apt description of business/government affairs. Wanting to convey a less ideological perspective and also to admit without apology our primitive understanding of the competitive issues we wished to address, our course had the acronym GROP, with a long *O*, to suggest that we were groping with complicated and poorly understood issues. I thank several classes of GROP students for their tolerance.

I would also like to thank several groups of midlevel executives at AT&T who a bit unwittingly helped to test and refine the concepts described here. During the period of this book's preparation, I conducted several seminars on the competitive effects of regulatory change as part of AT&T's executive education program. Each seminar was a test for the then current version of the outline of this book. Because these seminars occurred at a time when AT&T was itself undergoing unprecedented change in its regulatory environment, these audiences were both especially attentive and critical—an ideal combination for someone preparing this book.

There are numerous other individuals to thank as well. George Lockwood, the entrepreneur at Monterey Abalone Farms described in chapter 2, triggered a host of intellectual issues when he responded thoughtfully to a *Harvard Business Review* article I wrote in the late 1970s on business/government issues. He has continued to support my research efforts over the years by his willingness to allow his company to serve as a laboratory specimen.

Because this book brings together many ideas that I have considered over the past fifteen years, I am indebted to my collaborators in these prior research efforts, including William Abernathy, Edward Blanchard, Stephen Bradley, Mark Farber, David Garvin, Royce Ginn, David Harrison, José Gomez-Ibanez, Anne Hill, John Jackson, C. James Koch, Robert Larner, James Meehan, John R. Meyer, Stephen O'Connell, and Richard Startz.

I am also indebted to research assistants and case writers who helped in this project and the projects leading up to it, including Bram Johnson, Tim Greening, Rick Counihan, David Bell, Clint Oster, Ray Palmer, William Jackson, Richard Levitan, Jeffrey Hunker, and Reid Drucker.

Because this book rests so heavily on case materials, most of them distributed by HBS Case Services at the Graduate School of Business Administration at Harvard, I would also like to acknowledge the permission of the Business School to use the materials described here as well as the permission of those companies that assisted me in developing research and teaching materials on these important issues.

Martin Kessler and Sheila Friedling of Basic Books provided insightful comments and painless editing.

And my family left me alone to stare at the computer monitor as I tried to master the intellectual processing of words while simultaneously trying to master their physical processing. For the sake of my readers, I hope I did a better job at the former than at the latter.

PART I

UNDERSTANDING COMPETITION WHEN GOVERNMENT MATTERS

Chapter 1

The Iron Law

It is a simple fact: when doing business in the United States, government matters. It always has and it always will. So long as governments—liberal or conservative, small or large, efficient or wasteful—collect taxes, spend revenues, or pass laws, public actions will influence private profits.

For some businesses, profits increase when government acts; for others, profits fall. Who wins and who loses is by no means accidental; rather, it is the predictable consequence of the interaction among individuals, corporations, and political organizations that often knowingly and sometimes unwittingly take political and economic actions to shape these gains and losses.

While the process itself is complex, the outcome is not: every act of government, no matter what its broader merits or demerits for society at large, creates winners and losers within the competitive sector of the economy.[1] These gains and losses, which accrue to both individuals and corporations, become the object of intense political attention at the same time they help shape the nation's international competitiveness, impart a direction to its research and development programs, and generally help shape the direction and pattern of growth of our economic institutions. This outcome is so predictable that it constitutes virtually an Iron Law of Public Policy. A few examples will illustrate the Iron Law at work.

A governmental agency in California succeeds in its efforts to increase the population of the endangered sea otter. Ostensibly this has little to do with business interests. Not so. As a natural predator of abalone, the revival of the sea otter population disadvantages those abalone fishermen who harvest abalone from the sea. At the same time, a new competitive opportunity is created for those aquaculturists who cultivate abalone in tanks on land.[2]

A federal agency bans the use of fluorocarbon propellants in aerosol products to protect the upper atmosphere. The resulting shift in market shares for existing products and aerosol technologies places some multimillion-dollar financial enterprises in jeopardy but creates significant growth opportunities for others.[3]

The president of a modest-sized corporation comes to the White House to request "technical waivers" of certain allegedly onerous federal economic regulations. The deliberations never make the evening news, but a White House economist estimates that the granting of these waivers could add $5 billion to the net worth of this single corporation while adversely affecting a large number of the firm's competitors. The waivers are granted.[4]

Policy makers debate the merits and demerits of natural gas price decontrol with considerable attention to the estimated redistribution of perhaps $40 billion from gas consumers to gas producers. While politicians focus on the legitimate concerns for the equity or inequity of various gas-pricing policies, the international competitiveness of several U.S. industries hinges on the outcome of these debates.[5]

These are, of course, extreme examples. Abalone harvesting is not now one of the nation's major enterprises and is unlikely to become one; and not many public policies have the competitive significance of natural gas price decontrol. However, these are not isolated examples. Virtually every public policy has similar kinds of competitive implications. If as policy makers we are to succeed in designing programs to achieve our social and economic objectives in the most effective manner, we must appreciate the economic and political forces our actions set in motion. Similarly, if as business managers we are to do our jobs well and satisfy the interests of our stockholders, workers, and the society that granted us a corporate charter in the first place, we too must come to understand and deal effectively with the political and economic forces shaping competition.

Importance of Perspective

Despite the magnitude and pervasiveness of these competitive impacts, the consequences of public policy for competition remain poorly understood. One possible explanation is that policy makers are not engaged in managing competitive enterprises and private-sector decision makers are not engaged in the design of sound public policy. This book tries to join these two perspectives to show how an understanding of the competitive effects of government policy can contribute both to better decision making in the private sector and to wiser public policy.

A second possible reason why the consequences of public policy for competition remain poorly understood is that in our public debates over economic policy, we have become preoccupied with questions of macroeconomics: What should we do about the federal deficit? Is the money supply expanding too rapidly? Is Keynesian economics dead? Should "supply-siders" control federal fiscal policy?

There is no doubt about the importance of these large and important issues, yet somehow these macroeconomic policy discussions seem distant from the affairs of most of us. Whether as managers of corporations, as public policy makers, or individual citizens, the economic world we experience directly every day is the world of the microeconomy: individual enterprises competing in individual markets and dealing with individual public policy initiatives. Unless we are directly engaged in the banking sector, we are rarely confronted with larger-scale problems of the money supply; rather, the issue more immediate is an unexpected Occupational Safety and Health Administration (OSHA) safety inspector at the factory gate. While we might find conversation on the merits of supply-side economics intellectually stimulating, the arcane details of the tax code are likely to be as significant to our individual economic affairs.

In fact, the economic challenges most of us face are not at the macro level but at the level of individual industries and the individual companies and governmental agencies we manage. A booming U.S. economy is good for the country as a whole but does not guarantee a viable domestic steel industry. Technological advances in semiconductors are undoubtedly important to long-run worldwide economic growth, but they may mean little to domestic firms if the Japanese pick off one market at a time in a calculated policy of "targeting." The control of inflation will unquestionably benefit the nation as a whole but will do little to resolve the problems of the domestic agricultural industry, the declining shoe industry, or the troubled international banking sector.

Today there is an increasing need to address questions of microeconomic policy. During much of the 1970s this need was reflected in discussions of the "deregulation" of those industries long subjected to complex rules for pricing and competitive entry into new markets. These public deliberations have led to major reforms in the transportation, energy, telecommunications, and banking sectors, to cite just four examples. These reform efforts clearly reveal the nation's growing awareness of the need to deal with issues of economic policy at the level of individual industrial sectors.

Most recently this need to address issues of microeconomic policy has been reflected in debates over the pros and cons of what has come to be called "industrial policy."[6] Unfortunately, talk of centralized planning, picking winners and losers, allocating capital, and the like has distracted our attention from some real and unavoidable microeconomic issues—basically, from the fact that every act of government shapes competitive market institutions in important ways. Every act of government creates individual winners and losers in the marketplace. Every gain and loss triggers subsequent rounds of political action and reaction, with attendant consequences for international competitiveness and long-term economic growth. This process is relevant not merely to the so-called regulated industries or those "smokestack" and "high-tech" industries currently the focus of the industrial policy debate. Rather this dynamic political and economic process is at the heart of what we ought to be thinking about when we consider microeconomic policy for all industries.

The Limitations of an Ideological Perspective

Still a third reason we have yet to come to grips with the realities of competition when government matters is that too many of us have approached the issue a bit more ideologically and a bit less dispassionately than we might always admit.

Most of us have strong opinions on microeconomic policy issues. We all have our own plans to change regulatory practices, reform tax laws, and stimulate economic growth. We know what we would *like* government to do—or not to do—to protect economic freedoms, redress social inequities, and otherwise facilitate economic exchange. But what we would like government to do and what it is capable of doing are sometimes two different things. And in the area of microeconomic policy in particular, there are numerous unanswered questions regarding the role government *can* play in correcting market failures, facilitating efficient operation of a market economy, and generally contributing to economic growth. Our wishes notwithstanding, there is much ignorance as to the full range of microeconomic forces set in motion by governmental institutions.

Frankly, a good deal of this ignorance is convenient. It is convenient to political liberals because it often excuses them from coming to grips with some of the consequences of their well-intended, but sometimes misdirected, programs for public intervention into the affairs of business. It is similarly convenient for those who are politically conservative because ignorance can excuse them from coming to grips with the reality that government policy *does* shape competitive institutions in important ways—whether or not they like it, whether or not they acknowledge it, and whether or not policy makers manage it.

The Limits of Liberal Ideology

A fundamental limitation of the liberal perspective on business/government relationships is that often goals are confused with outcomes.[7] To many liberals the imposition of a government regulation or "industrial policy" is tantamount to attaining the objectives the policy was designed to achieve. In this conception of the world of political economy, virtue is on the side of the intervenor. Never mind that the excessive stringency of the nation's water pollution control laws has not yielded clean water but has caused environmental damage to ambient air quality. Never mind that rules designed to protect the interests of consumers often result in costly red tape and further consumer expense. Never mind that well-intended policies of subsidy and protection often create a dependence on the part of business and labor on continued government intervention and support.

The mistaken equation of political goals with economic outcomes stems from a common liberal failure to address four realities. The first reality is simply that government regulations, like the market systems they are designed to improve upon, are never perfect. Thus the initial efforts to regulate the flammability of children's sleepwear resulted in the regulation-induced use of TRIS, a chemical subsequently withdrawn when it was discovered to cause cancer.[8] Or in another case, an analyst has recently shown that emissions controls on new automobiles have become so stringent that consumers have deferred purchases of new cars and kept older, dirtier cars on the road longer —to such an extent that the air today may actually be dirtier than it would have been if less stringent, and consequently less costly, demands had been placed on automakers.[9]

Similarly, many liberal advocates of trade restraint in troubled industries like the auto and steel industries have argued their positions on the grounds that these enterprises *deserve* the nation's help. These proponents ignore the fact that such "help" often encourages foreign competitors to upgrade the products they sell in the United States, export more finished goods, invest in U.S. manufacturing plants, and take other strategic actions, the consequences of which are often detrimental to the very interests trade restraint was supposed to protect. Japanese auto producers, for example, increased their dollar volume of sales in the United States by 50 percent, or over $4 billion annually, during four years of trade restraint. They did this by using import limitations to shore up prices and to finance aggressive moves into high-priced and high-profit market segments. This restraint, of course, was hardly to the long-term benefit of domestic producers, no matter how "deserving" of protection they might have been.[10]

One example of the confusion of goals with their outcomes occurred in this author's classroom. The students were examining proposed standards to save energy by increasing the fuel efficiency of home air conditioners. The analysis suggested that the greater fuel efficiency of the regulated appliances might actually encourage more air conditioner use and hence greater energy consumption than otherwise. This result could occur because more fuel-efficient appliances, once purchased, had low costs of incremental operation. Thus a consumer who had already paid three to four hundred dollars for a highly efficient air conditioner might as well use it intensively to get his or her money's worth. This, of course, was not the objective of the proposed policy. In frustration one student blurted out, "But that's not what's supposed to happen!"

These imperfections in the political and regulatory process are neither surprising nor unpredictable. All institutions have their weaknesses, and government is no exception. Yet all too often debates over the merits and demerits of public intervention are conducted as if the choice were between an imperfect market and a perfect governmental alternative. The reality, of course, is that the choice is between imperfect markets and imperfect government rules. To identify the imperfections and limits—as well as the potential benefits—of public intervention, it is necessary to look at the indirect competitive consequences of public action. We need to move beyond wishful thinking to thoughtful analysis of how competitive private-sector institutions are shaped by public policy.

The second reality that liberals often ignore is the long-term effect of government intervention. Most studies of the effectiveness of public policies are what economists call "partial equilibrium" analyses—that is, they look at the impacts of policy while holding everything else constant. Thus when policy makers for the state of California look at the prospect for a unitary tax—a tax levied on the worldwide earnings of companies with facilities in California—the tax might look very attractive. Such a tax, however, appears very different when it is recognized that, in the long run, companies have the option of *not* locating in California. Or a policy of rent control might look attractive to a big-city mayor—so long as the consequences for subsequent investments in housing are ignored. The problem, of course, is that everything else is not constant. There is a pressing need to look beyond the immediate effects of public intervention to their long-term consequences.

Indeed, there is a need to look beyond individual policy interventions to see what kinds of strategic changes take place when policy makers intervene in a competitive setting. Take federal regulation of the automobile. Air pollution control requirements are uniform for every vehicle, which has the effect of encouraging manufacturers to produce a relatively homogeneous fleet of lightweight, fuel-efficient vehicles. Federal energy standards, in contrast, are based on fleet averages. This policy actively encourages fleet diversity but fuel-efficient design. Safety regulations are based on the physical design of the vehicle itself and not its actual performance on the road. Accordingly, larger, more crash-resistant but less fuel-efficient construction is encouraged. These safety rules and regulations take little account of the entire fleet-mix question.

The point here is not merely that safety, environmental goals, and fuel-economy goals are necessarily in competition with one another. Of course they are. Rather the point is that the failure to coordinate the various federal policies to achieve these objectives results in *unnecessarily* conflicting and costly regulation.

Still a fourth limitation of the liberal perspective on business/government interaction is that it tends to ignore the fact that competition is itself a very powerful form of regulation. In many ways the currently popular term deregulation is a misnomer. The substitution of market regulatory forces for government regulatory mechanisms may be *deregulation* in popular parlance but not necessarily in reality.

The failure to treat competition as a regulatory force is not without its costs. For one thing, the omission encourages more government intervention than might otherwise be desirable. Substituting political and regulatory forces with their unknown consequences for market forces with relatively well understood effects is troubling in itself. But even more important, the *mixture* of governmental and market regulatory forces is poorly understood. As evidence of this, consider the task of any senior manager of a regional telephone-operating company who is trying to cope with unfamiliar competitive forces unleashed by the breakup of AT&T while simultaneously constrained by the regulatory actions of public utility commissions. At first look the problem is unfamiliar competition. Yet a second look suggests that competition by itself is hardly a problem—although admittedly a challenge. Many people are experienced in competitive markets, if not already working in the operating companies themselves then available as consultants or new employees. The real problem is the need to deal simultaneously with regulated markets in one segment of activities and competitive forces in the other. This is not a skill in which many managers or regulators are currently proficient.

There is a clear need to better understand how the self-regulating forces of the marketplace operate in a world in which government intervention takes place, because increasingly industry is subjected to both forms of restraint simultaneously.

The Limits of Conservative Ideology

If the liberal perspective on the business/government relationship has its limits, so too does the conservative perspective. Perhaps its major limitation is its frequent preoccupation with the immediate and tangible cost to business of government intervention. There is no doubt that the costs of such intervention in the affairs of business are central to any analysis of its merits and consequences, yet too limited a definition of costs can be terribly misleading.

A narrow conception of costs ignores the impact that government intervention can have on management discretion. For example, the real burden of public actions is often not measured by excessive costs today but by the loss of managerial flexibility tomorrow. Indeed one of the major "costs" of governmental restrictions on management—the distraction of management time and attention from efforts to improve productivity, develop new processes, and market new products—is typically ignored in exercises designed to measure the cost of government intervention. Without arguing the merits of auto emissions control, there is still the question of what the opportunity cost was in forgone technological innovation as a consequence of diverting hundreds of thousands of research hours to emissions control problems rather than to other aspects of automotive technology. It is even possible to argue that this opportunity cost was so great that air quality actually suffered. (This might be the case if, preoccupied with regulatory compliance, engineers failed to develop some radically new, nonpolluting automotive technology.) At the other extreme, it is possible to argue that the opportunity cost of emissions regulation was actually negative in that the auto emissions problem gave the industry a head start on subsequent innovations in automotive electronics. Whether the indirect consequences were good or bad, they should be part of the analysis of this public policy initiative.

A narrow focus on cost similarly ignores issues of consumer welfare. An excellent case in point involves arguments for and against the imposition of mandatory deposits on soft-drink containers to reduce litter. The reduction in roadside litter is clearly a desirable social objective; so the question quickly arises whether the consequences of imposing regulation justify the benefit. As typically occurs, conservative opponents of intervention focus on the program's cost. Not unexpectedly, liberal advocates of regulation turn this line of argument on its head and note that returnable containers deliver soft drinks at a lower cost per ounce than one-way (disposable) containers. They conclude that the regulation not only cleans up the environment but saves the consumer money as well. The counterargument is typically that these cost estimates are wrong— that costs would, in fact, rise.

Rarely do either proponents or opponents look to the deeper issue of consumer welfare. In the state of Oregon, for example, the average price of soft drinks appears to have fallen after the imposition of container regulation,[11] to a level just above that of soft drinks formerly sold in returnable containers. The cost of returnables had risen because some convenience-oriented consumers threw away returnable containers rather than recycling them. The price was, nonetheless, well below the earlier price for soft drinks sold in one-way packages and thus, on average, was lower than before regulation. Ostensibly the advocates of regulation had won their argument: there was less litter, and consumers' out-of-pocket costs for soft drinks had fallen. According to this cost-oriented analysis, the reduction in litter had been achieved at a negative cost.

But look at the same question from a consumer welfare perspective. Prior to the imposition of regulation, some consumers chose to buy nonreturnable containers, which cost more than returnables. Presumably the large price differential was justified by the added convenience. After regulation the convenience was gone, and the out-of-pocket savings with returnables was even less than it was before—since the price of returnables had increased. In other words, consumers who previously purchased soft drinks packaged in one-way containers were worse off than before: they lost the convenience they valued highly but received reductions in price less than they could have received previously had they been willing to sacrifice convenience. Of course, these consumers did not have to sacrifice convenience entirely if they chose not to. They could simply throw away and not recycle a very costly and socially valuable returnable container—hardly an outcome advocates of regulation had in mind.

Now consider former and current users of returnables. They still used returnables but purchased fewer soft drinks due to the higher price. They were clearly worse off than before. In truth, both classes of consumers were worse off after the regulation than before it despite the fact that the average price of soft drinks had fallen. A narrow analysis of cost, which ignored consumer welfare issues, could easily miss this important result.

By the way, the conclusion of this analysis is not that it was a mistake to impose restrictions on soft-drink containers in Michigan. To the contrary, even though citizens, as soft-drink consumers, might have been worse off with regulation, as members of society as a whole, they might well have been better off because of the reduction in litter. It all depends on how the public valued litter reduction versus consumer convenience. The point is not to argue for or against container regulation but to observe that the proper answer to the question of whether such regulation was desirable will not be found by looking solely at the out-of-pocket costs of public action. It is essential to look beyond costs to the full set of social and economic consequences of governmental intervention in competitive markets.

Still another limit of the conservative perspective on business/government relationships is the implicit denial that government matters. One need not disagree with the conservative political notion that the government which governs least is the government which governs best to recognize that whatever government there is will have major impacts on competitive economic institutions.

The conservative dilemma is that the mere acknowledgment that government has an unavoidable impact on business is an invitation for policy makers to manage that impact. To avoid the political consequences of such conscious public decisions regarding the economy and to avoid results they might otherwise find distasteful, conservatives often deny the existence of the effect or focus their attention on macroeconomic policy issues. The former is not unlike the practice of killing the messenger who brought bad news; it discourages others from bearing bad news but hardly denies the unreported tragedies. The latter response partly explains the enthusiasm of conservatives for supply-side macropolicies and their aversion to the very concept of industrial policy.

In fairness, both the liberal and conservative perspectives just described are stylized myths and hence a bit exaggerated. Not all programs of government intervention are motivated by naïve liberal expectations of complete success, nor is the opposition to intervention motivated solely by a myopic conservative preoccupation with costs. The exaggerations notwithstanding, there is considerable truth to these caricatures of current approaches to business/government affairs. There is a pressing need to expand our analyses beyond good intentions and narrow conceptions of cost to consider carefully both the practical limits and practical consequences of government intervention in the affairs of business. We need a better understanding of competition when government matters.

The Need for Better Understanding

This book is a direct response to the need to better understand the competitive effects of government action. At present there is a substantial gap between the approaches undertaken by policy analysts and by business analysts in evaluating government's impacts. Effective understanding of the problems of each party requires an appreciation of the other's point of view. The failure to recognize the factors determining the competitive outcomes of public policy decisions and the identity of those who win and those who lose as a consequence of those decisions will prevent managers in both public and private sectors from making more effective future decisions.

Consequently this book is aimed both at managers in the private sector and policy makers in the public sector. Subsequent chapters will not only describe the economic and political consequences of government action, they will also identify strategies for dealing with the political and competitive realities of government policy. These strategies are intended to allow us all to attain a richer, more profitable and socially responsible level of economic performance.

This book is also a direct response to the need to address issues of business/government interaction less ideologically and more dispassionately. Thus, while primarily aimed at practicing managers and policy makers, this volume may also be helpful to analysts. In particular, it should help management scientists who need to develop a more sophisticated appreciation and more rigorous analytical methods for measuring the effects of government policy on business. It should also help policy analysts who recognize the need to appreciate better the full range of consequences of the programs they advocate.

There are two ways we could reduce our ignorance and improve our current understanding of the dynamic competitive consequences of governmental action. The first would be to get on with the task of experimenting with new governmental initiatives to determine just how they work. This might be an intellectually attractive option were it not for the human and economic costs of mistakes. Whether motivated by liberal or conservative political ideals, social experimentation is not an avenue to pursue casually.

Fortunately there is a second and far less painful method, one that relies on the fact that we have already conducted a large number of "natural experiments" on the role government plays in shaping competitive institutions. This experimental evidence is the product of decades of government regulation and policy intervention. This book examines some of the evidence on the historical impact of government actions on competitive enterprises in the hope that the lessons from the past will help us better understand the nature of competition when government matters.

Despite an earlier warning that a focus on the cost of government intervention can be misleading, this book begins with an examination of the costs attributable to government intervention. The focus, however, is not on the total cost burden of government actions. There will be no attempt to discuss the aggregate costs of government intervention to show that they are either higher or lower than conventionally believed. The issue to be addressed is not whether we have either too much or too little government control of the economy. Rather my purpose is to examine the competitive effects of government policy generally and not to evaluate the wisdom of individual regulatory programs per se. Thus this discussion of costs will focus not on aggregate costs but on costs as viewed from the perspective of individual competitive enterprises.

For example, many environmental regulations add to the cost of doing business.[12] However, those firms with the lowest cost increases can actually benefit competitively from these cost increases since their competitors are affected so adversely.[13] Other government requirements, in contrast, actually reduce the cost of doing business, perhaps by constraining competitors from producing certain goods or services. The fluorocarbon ban cited earlier, by prohibiting the high-cost aerosol technology and thus fundamentally constraining the industry's "production function," may well have lowered the costs of production in the toiletries industry.[14] But like policy-induced cost increases, these cost decreases did not affect all competitors equally. Those individual firms experiencing the largest cost reductions benefited more than their competition. Stated differently, whether costs go up or down, the Iron Law is still at work.

Not only do costs vary among competitors due to governmental actions, but the composition of costs changes with policy. For example, many environmental regulations require large capital expenditures. These increase the fixed costs of doing business and thus make individual competitors more vulnerable to the volume declines associated with downswings in the business cycle.[15]

Other public actions shift costs among segments of an industry. For example, the regulations cited earlier requiring soft-drink containers to carry deposits make soft-drink distribution even more labor-intensive than it would otherwise be. This can affect the relative competitive position of soft-drink bottlers who have a comparative advantage in managing labor-intensive activities as opposed to concentrate and syrup manufacturers whose competitive strength is usually in access to capital and mass advertising. Regulations mandating passive restraints in automobiles can significantly affect risks in the insurance industry by lowering bodily injury claims and, thus, the insurance component of driving costs. There is generally little discussion of these questions in public policy debates, yet their impacts are often at the heart of the important competitive effects of public policy actions.

Subsequent chapters will also address the competitive effects that result from the strategic vulnerability of individual firms to changes in public policy. Let us reconsider the passive restraint example. Manufacturers of vehicles designed for two passengers in the front seat face a far different problem than do those with cars designed for three passengers. Relatively simple seat-belt systems can be used in the two-passenger seats, but more costly and complex systems are needed to protect three passengers.[16] This strategic impact is not unlike that which confronted auto makers when emissions controls were first imposed. General Motors specialized in the catalytic converter technology eventually embraced by regulators, while Chrysler specialized in electronic technologies that the regulatory authorities rejected as inadequate.[17]

Government actions often yield winners and losers by creating capital gains and losses for existing investments. Natural gas price decontrol, by possibly creating higher gas prices, might lower the resale value of a gas-heated house.[18] Strict "new source performance standards" that require new facilities to meet tougher requirements than old factories have to increase the value of existing plant and equipment in much the same way that tough auto emissions standards in the early 1970s created a premium for late-model used cars that lacked the expensive and performance-reducing emissions control equipment.[19] Part I describes these effects and documents their economic and political significance using actual case studies.

Part I concludes with an examination of the impact of public policy on productive capacity. Chapters 5 and 6 show how government actions can cause firms to rationalize existing capacity—sometimes through the extreme action of closing facilities, but more often through the far less visible means of adjusting the balance of various production processes in multistage manufacturing operations. This "rebalancing" activity can shift the bottlenecks in industry, alter the managerial skills required for efficient operation, and even shift the locus of the most profitable activities within a complex production and distribution chain.[20] For example, environmental restrictions on coke oven emissions have helped make coke production so costly and so discouraged capital investment in this aspect of steelmaking that this process is now the bottleneck operation in many integrated steelmaking facilities.

This book also examines the changes in the relative competitive position of new and existing facilities that are created by "grandfather" regulatory provisions which mandate less stringent requirements for old plants.[21] While the political rationale for such differentials is easily understood, the profound competitive implications often are not. This examination of the impact of government policy on the nation's production capacity differs from macroeconomic considerations that tend to focus on the problem of "crowding out"—that is, the diversion of capital from so-called productive investments to "compliance" investments. This study examines the phenomenon strictly from a corporate perspective to show how public actions can influence the scale, location, and timing of investments in new facilities and influence investors to modify, expand, or close existing plants.

To put all these competitive effects in their appropriate political context, Part II examines and describes the regulatory process and the responses of various parties to it. It is in this context that competitors can seek to alter the consequences of public action. This process is highly political in that it is very responsive to issues of fairness; it tends to be procedural, often to the point where procedural regularity matters as much as policy outcome; and, for a variety of political and organizational reasons, it often tends to be myopic in its perception of the relevant issues and time horizons.[22] These factors, in turn, all have competitive implications.

Because both competition and public policy making are dynamic processes, it is also important to describe the response of affected businesses to government intervention. There appears to be a significant difference between management's first reaction to government programs and its subsequent reactions. Initial reactions often tend to be ideological, sometimes demonstrating a lack of institutional sophistication. They frequently understate the competitive significance of public policies.

With experience, however, both managers and policy makers tend to be more sophisticated. Having recognized the significance of government policy and experienced the political process, they seek to manage regulatory uncertainty, influence the process, and ultimately exploit public actions for strategic competitive gain.[23] Part II demonstrates that competitive and political exploitation of governmental processes need not be antisocial—indeed, if properly understood and managed, competitive forces can be used to advance the broader goals of society as well as more specific goals of enterprise. It shows, in other words, the extent to which competitive interests and public objectives can be combined to avoid the beggar-thy-neighbor characteristics of so many current discussions of business/government issues.

Growing sophistication on the part of managers, of course, has implications for policy makers. Accordingly chapter 11 examines some of the challenges confronting policy makers as business becomes more sophisticated in dealing with public agencies. In particular, the risks of incremental decision making and the limits of cooperation in a political process where private managers control much of the relevant data are discussed.[24]

And finally, this book concludes with recommendations to both private-sector managers and public-sector policy makers on how to deal with the public's interest in a more sophisticated approach to microeconomic policy making. This approach will show managers in the private sector how awareness of and active participation in the political process can further the aims of enterprise in a socially responsible way. And it will demonstrate to policy makers in the public sector how anticipation of the competitive and strategic reactions of business to public policy initiatives can be used to advance social goals without unnecessarily constraining economic activity and private initiative. In sum, this book tries to unite the interests of decision makers in both the private and the public sectors by illuminating the important avenues of interaction between the competitive forces in one sector and the political forces in the other.

This is not a topic that will go away. The growing interdependence of national economies, combined with the inherent limitations of macroeconomic policy, makes it likely that government will become more active, not less, in its effort to shape economic growth. Whatever ideological form such policies ultimately take, they will likely fail if they are not designed with an explicit understanding of the realities of competition when government matters. Even the Reagan Administration, as committed as it is to policies aimed at getting government "off the back of business," can do so only with institutional changes.[25] These changes—indeed, any policy changes—will have significant competitive consequences and will create winners and losers in the marketplace. In other words, there is no escaping the Iron Law.

Chapter 2

The Pervasive Phenomenon

At 9:30 A.M. on August 8, 1975, George Lockwood, general partner and co-founder of the Monterey Abalone Farms, was considering the effects of the pervasive nature of government regulation on his efforts to get his new company off the ground.[1]

So begins a Harvard Business School case study on government regulation of business. The case continues:

[Forty-two different] local, state and federal government agencies were involved in the regulation of his business. While the regulations were sometimes burdensome . . . they did not constitute a serious impediment to the development of the company. Mr. Lockwood was concerned, however, that as his company completed the transition from primarily research activities to production activities, regulation would have an even larger impact. In the midst of these thoughts, Mr. Lockwood was informed that two inspectors from the California Division of Industrial Safety (CAL/OSHA) were at the front door seeking access to his facility.

Monterey Abalone Farms was in the business of growing, processing and selling abalone products in world markets. The abalone is a marine shellfish . . . related to oysters, clams, and scallops. In nature, it crawls along rocks on the ocean floor and feeds by scraping marine plants off the rocks and by grasping and eating floating kelp leaves.

At Monterey Abalone Farms, abalone were grown in tanks on land under tightly controlled environmental conditions. Whatever difficulties Monterey had with governmental authorities, they were matched by the technical challenge of abalone culture.

Lockwood's method of growing abalone was still experimental, but in 1975 success seemed just over the horizon. The initial research and development (R&D) efforts had been successful as had been the efforts to finance the fledgling company. The only obstacle in the way appeared to be the roadblocks created by government red tape.

> The two CAL/OSHA inspectors who arrived at Monterey Abalone Farms on the morning of August 8, 1975, requested access to the facility for the purpose of making an inspection. They stated that the Monterey Department of Health had informed them that a "serious ozone hazard" existed in the "abalone breathing room."
>
> Monterey Abalone Farms had a policy of restricting access to its facility . . . to protect the security of proprietary information and trade secrets. After verifying the identify of the inspectors and checking with legal counsel, Lockwood reluctantly admitted the inspectors.

Lockwood's reluctance stemmed both from his concern for proprietary information and from the fact that his facility did not have an "abalone breathing room." Ironically, once inside his facility, the inspectors acknowledged that Lockwood's lack of such a room was matched by their own lack of ozone monitoring equipment. Not surprisingly, this declaration did not add to Lockwood's peace of mind.

During this initial inspection the inspectors noted fourteen violations of a nonserious nature and issued appropriate citations and fines. Some of the citations were simple to correct: the failure to post a mandatory CAL/OSHA notice, for example. Other violations posed a more serious problem. One involved the alleged failure to properly ground an electric typewriter. Lockwood, in response to this citation, observed that the typewriter in question was grounded by means of a three-prong electrical plug. When he brought this to the attention of state authorities, they agreed that there was no violation, but to have the citation removed he would have to lodge an appeal nonetheless. Lockwood's frustrations were only partly soothed when he learned that a fellow California businessperson had been cited and forced to appeal the failure to ground a *manual* typewriter.[2]

One of the violations cited by inspectors proved to be much more than a technical or bureaucratic matter. It concerned the use of plastic-sheathed electrical cables installed in the roof and ceiling trusses of the building in 1969; at that time such wiring conformed with local building codes. Standards in use by CAL /OSHA in 1975, however, prohibited the use of such cable. Apparently, an industrial accident that had occurred after the original standard was put in place encouraged officials to insist on a more stringent standard. Of course, such standard tightening, as a public display that the government had "done something" in the aftermath of a tragic event, is not at all uncommon. Lockwood estimated that to remedy this single alleged violation would cost between $20,000 and $40,000.

While in the broader scheme of American business, $20,000 to $40,000 might appear a relatively small sum, financing that amount of electrical changes for Monterey Abalone Farms would require Lockwood to reduce his company's scientific staff by one-third, thus jeopardizing the company's research progress and subsequent stages of finance. In other words, this unanticipated expenditure could place in jeopardy the continued existence of the fledgling enterprise.

Lockwood was in a real bind. He could comply with the citation, but only by reducing his research effort. Alternatively, he could appeal the citation—with no assurance of success—and lose a considerable amount of his personal time and possibly the appeal as well. It appeared to be a no-win situation.

Government Is More than Regulation

As Lockwood contemplated his choices, he began to direct his attention to the other ways in which government policy shaped the nature of his business. It was becoming quite clear that ignorance of regulatory affairs could be as serious an impediment to the success of his business as inadequate technology. He did not need very many $20,000 to 40,000 challenges to do him in, whatever the objective merits of his case.

This reflection led him to conclude that, in fact, government involvement in his business was a pervasive phenomenon. It became clear that in many ways the very existence of his business was a consequence of various successes and failures in the public policy arena. For example, the market for abalone represented such an attractive financial opportunity in part because environmental programs aimed at the preservation of the endangered sea otter had been successful. The sea otter is a natural predator of the abalone; the revival of the sea otter population meant a decrease in abalone available for fishermen.

The profitability of abalone farming depended on the size of the market for this high-priced delicacy. Prior to 1968, it had been illegal to ship abalone harvested in California out of the state, but the state legislature had eliminated this restriction, thus opening up to entrepreneurs like George Lockwood the large and well-established Far East abalone market.

The government's impact on the demand for abalone was not limited to export or environmental policies. Among the potential customers for abalone was the California Fish and Game Authority, which might be expected to purchase substantial numbers of young abalone breeding stock to help replenish deficient natural supplies. The government, in other words, had a pervasive impact on the demand for abalone.

Government's impact on Lockwood's business was by no means confined to the demand side of the market, however. Various policies of the state and federal government had similarly profound impacts on both Monterey Abalone Farms itself and its prospective competitors.

At the very same time that Lockwood was concerned with the CAL/OSHA inspectors, researchers at the University of California, working under the auspices of the National Sea Grant Program of the U.S. Department of Commerce, were attempting to reproduce, at public expense, abalone aquaculture technology. Ironically, when Lockwood had applied to this same agency for assistance in his research efforts, he had been turned down. Compounding this irony was the fact that a former employee of Monterey Abalone Farms had been hired to assist in this publicly funded R&D effort. There was little question that success in the development of this competitive alternative could have major implications for Lockwood's enterprise.

While direct financial assistance to Lockwood had not been forthcoming from the government, it would be misleading to ignore indirect financial assistance. Raising capital for development of an unproven technology that always seemed to be three to four years away from yielding a marketable product was expectedly difficult, but Monterey Abalone Farms had been greatly assisted in the financing effort by various provisions of the Federal Tax Code that allowed investors to justify commitment of substantial assets to risky R&D projects with long lead times. Even this assistance, of course, was not without strings attached. Lockwood had faced major regulatory restrictions on his efforts to solicit potential investors in the abalone enterprise.

The company had also been supported indirectly by the very same University of California system that was now its potential competitor. After all, highly trained and technologically sophisticated marine biologists, the supply of which was essential to the success of Lockwood's enterprise, were the product of state and federal education programs.

In going through the list of government impacts on his business, George Lockwood came to appreciate more fully than ever before the extent of "government involvement"—a term he preferred to government regulation—in the affairs of his business. Prior to his experience with the CAL/OSHA inspectors, Lockwood had paid very little systematic attention to the impact of government policy on his business. Given his most recent reflections, he was unlikely to have this same view again.

A Quick Study

Lockwood's story is one of much success tempered by occasional failures. The initial safety citations at his plant were formally appealed. The most onerous allegations, including the wiring problem, were overturned. Lockwood's subsequent dealings with OSHA authorities occurred not only in his own plant but in the hearing rooms in which decisions regarding future safety regulations were made. Lockwood apparently learned enough to decide that never again would he merely react to safety regulations; rather, it was essential to the success of his business that he anticipate the development of new rules and procedures that helped shape the marketplace in which he competed, if for no other reason than to gain an edge on his competition, who, of course, had to deal with these same regulatory authorities. Lockwood had discovered what all business executives who confront government eventually discover: you did not have to run General Motors to have a direct stake in public policy.

Lockwood also responded directly to the challenge of competition from the University of California. He sought and successfully obtained a permanent court injunction prohibiting his former employee from working in the field of abalone aquaculture.

And while it required literally hundreds of hours of his time, he successfully influenced federal authorities to redirect the Sea Grant funds at the university to noncompetitive activities. It took him so much time because he made several false starts in his political efforts, trying first to reason with Executive Branch administrators and then appealing more successfully to influential congressional representatives on basic issues of jobs, fairness, and wasteful government expenditures—three "magic words" in the halls of Congress.

While George Lockwood was a quick study and came to deal successfully with many aspects of government involvement in his business, his efforts were not without both their risks and frustrations. He spent more than six months acquiring environmental permits, for example, for his new industrial activity. Because Monterey Abalone Farms was breaking new technological ground unfamiliar to many of the environmental regulators, Lockwood was forced to pose his problem not merely to state environmental authorities but directly to the Environmental Protection Agency (EPA) in Washington. In the process of these deliberations there were major setbacks at the plant site itself, including one snafu that cost the young firm a full year's delay in bringing abalone to the marketplace. Given the massive burden of government regulation on George Lockwood's time, it is almost impossible to know what kinds of technological and entrepreneurial opportunities were missed as he dealt with the public bureaucracy.

Lockwood's success in the late 1970s can be viewed as evidence of the vitality of our current system of business and government interaction. After all, he ultimately did prevail and today his business is prosperous. Alternatively, his experience can be viewed as evidence of the persistence, skill, and even luck that can be required for entrepreneurs to cope successfully with today's government bureaucracy. Whichever of these lessons one wishes to derive from the experiences of Monterey Abalone Farms, there is no escaping the observation that government involvement in the affairs of Lockwood's enterprise was pervasive.

Lockwood again confronted this reality in the early 1980s. As his business was developing, his scientists discovered that abalone would grow much more rapidly if fed a diet of specially grown kelp. Harvesting this kelp would require special permits from state authorities. This time George Lockwood did not receive the needed permits, but he had learned how to play the game. When the state of California presented him with obstacles, Lockwood approached the state of Hawaii to see what economic development interests it might have in the new industry of abalone aquaculture. Officials there agreed to facilitate Lockwood's efforts to grow kelp offshore were he to move his facility. Lockwood accepted their offer—once again demonstrating the pervasive impact of government on his business.

George Lockwood's experience is not unique. While the ways in which government can shape the affairs of business will vary greatly from case to case, it is likely that a thoughtful analysis of virtually any other industrial activity in the U.S. economy would identify a similar list of government policies with significant impacts on competition. Government *is* a pervasive phenomenon.

George Lockwood Is Not Alone

It is also true that many of the competitive effects of public policy are both unintended and indirect. During deliberations over the Endangered Species Act, for example, there was no consideration of the competitive implications for abalone farmers. Similarly, the indirect impact of Federal Sea Grant programs to encourage research in aquaculture technology at the University of California was likely to influence Lockwood's business at least as much and probably more than any OSHA regulation.

Not only was government policy a pervasive influence on Lockwood's business, but its consequences were complex. OSHA increased the cost of doing business. The overhead burden of government regulation on Lockwood's time also increased the fixed costs of the enterprise. Regulatory obstacles to the new firm's development contributed to what industrial economists call "barriers to entry," thereby limiting the aquaculture industry's total productive capacity and decreasing the degree of competition within the industry.

As subsequent chapters will show, Lockwood's case is, in many respects, a simple one. In one competitive setting after another, the impacts of government policy on the costs of doing business, the cost structure of business, and productive capacity are major determinants of the competitive environment in which U.S. firms operate. It is these impacts to which we now turn.

Chapter 3

Government and the Cost

of Doing Business

This chapter explores the impact of government on the cost of doing business. From an economic perspective, of course, cost changes are important in their own right. But because cost impacts are the most visible consequences of public policy for business firms, they take on an added political significance. The combination of these economic and political realities ultimately determines who profits when government intervenes in business affairs. By examining the impact of public actions on industrial costs and identifying some of the political and competitive implications of these cost changes, we will be better equipped to understand competition when government matters.

Increased Costs

No one will be surprised to know that in most cases, regulations and other governmental rules increase the costs of doing business. After all, when the government requires businesses to do things they would not otherwise choose to do—provide a particular type of product label, treat an industrial effluent, or conduct business in a certain way—we would logically expect it to increase costs. If costs fell with these actions, business would not usually need the prodding of government to do them.

Whether or not these higher costs are truly onerous is often hard to determine. Have, for example, tamper-proof package requirements really required over-the-counter medicine manufacturers to do more than they would otherwise have done on their own in the face of the Tylenol murders?[1] It is not hard to see, however, that to do more costs more, and, ultimately, that is the reason that government intervention usually costs business and consumers money.

When government is not asking business to do more, it is often asking it to do less, and that can cost money too. Many government requirements prohibit certain activities because they have some antisocial consequences not otherwise fully accounted for in the firm's decision making, be it pollution, social injustice, risk of accident in the home, or the like. Recognizing that business is not malevolent and intentionally antisocial, these consequences are typically the result of competitors' efforts to minimize the costs of doing business. By definition, government prohibitions of this sort force business to employ higher-cost—albeit more socially acceptable—production methods.

In individual cases, these cost increases can be sizable. Robert Crandall of the Brookings Institution has estimated that automotive emissions, vehicle safety, and fuel economy regulations have increased the cost of automotive services from less than $200 per car in 1972 to nearly $2,000 per car by the early 1980s.[2] Pollution controls have added 2 to 3 percent to the cost of the paper on which this book is printed.[3] And the tamper-resistant packaging requirements referred to a moment ago have added 2 to 3 cents to the cost of a bottle of aspirin and its substitutes.

In the aggregate, these cost increases are even more substantial. Murray Weidenbaum, former chairman of President Reagan's Council of Economic Advisers, has estimated that for the economy as a whole, the cost increases associated with government regulation were over $103 billion dollars in 1979—a sum that, with inflation, would exceed $141 billion in 1985 dollars —or more than $600 per capita.[4] Obviously, the cost increases associated with governmental actions are significant.

Decreased Costs

But it is important to stress that not all government rules increase costs. Some actually lower the cost of doing business. In fact, some governmental rules and requirements have such obviously beneficial impacts in this regard that most of us have long since ceased to call them "regulations" at all. Basic laws of incorporation, contract, truthful information reporting, and so forth, impose strict rules and constraints on business behavior but clearly serve both the interests of enterprise and the public by reducing uncertainty, limiting risk, and codifying business procedures. These all serve to lower costs.

The Fluorocarbon Ban

Even more recent rules of the kind we still call "regulation" can reduce cost. An example was the Environmental Protection Agency's ban of fluorocarbon propellants in aerosol sprays several years ago.[5] The extensive use of these chemicals was forbidden after two scientists published an article postulating that fluorocarbons were depleting the ozone levels in the stratosphere. Lower ozone levels, by allowing more ultraviolet radiation to reach the earth, they argued, would increase the incidence of skin cancer and might have other detrimental environmental effects. According to the theory, the inert fluorocarbons could exist freely in the environment for over a hundred years. Over time, they would migrate upward into the stratosphere, some six miles above the earth's surface. There, ultraviolet radiation would break down the fluorocarbon molecules, causing them to emit chlorine atoms, which would convert tens of thousands of ozone molecules into ordinary oxygen in a catalytic reaction.

Because of wide natural variation in the ozone level, the thesis was almost impossible to test directly. Thus the dilemma facing the regulatory authorities at the EPA was that there existed a plausible argument that a serious environmental hazard existed, but by the time any such hypothesis might be scientifically documented, the damage would already have been done.

Compounding the scientific problem was an economic one: to avoid an uncertain environmental problem would impose quite certain economic costs. Fluorocarbons were an important ingredient in many consumer products, including personal deodorants and hairspray. The decision to ban their use would, therefore, presumably hinge on the trade-off of these economic costs with the environmental risks.

Accordingly, government consultants were asked how much these regulations would cost to implement. The analysts began by doing the obvious: they looked at the alternative methods for packaging hairspray, antiperspirants, and other cosmetics. The difference between the (presumably higher) costs of these methods, when compared to the fluorocarbon option, would represent the cost of regulation against which the uncertain hazard had to be measured.

What the consultants discovered was that virtually all the relevant alternative packaging options were actually cheaper. An antiperspirant, for example, that could be delivered in an aerosol package for 71 cents could be delivered in a mechanical pump bottle for only 46 cents. They also discovered, however, that few competitors were willing to adopt the alternative low-cost packaging technologies for fear consumers would rush to purchase the products delivered in the traditional fashion by their competitors.[6]

Given these competitive pressures, it was unlikely that fluorocarbons would disappear from the cosmetics counter through voluntary action even if socially conscious management shared the environmentalists' concern for the potential depletion of the earth's ozone layer. Or if they did disappear, the uncertainty regarding competitive changes in the process would be substantial—and all for a highly uncertain environmental benefit.

The EPA was able to resolve the problem when it recognized that production costs might actually decline with a ban on the use of fluorocarbons. Yet concerns regarding competitive reaction and market share might well prevent profit-sensitive managements from abandoning fluorocarbons voluntarily. EPA analysts concluded that a voluntary ban would be ineffective, but a mandatory ban might be tolerable.[7]

The Prisoners' Dilemma

The federal authorities had happened upon a "prisoners' dilemma."[8] In the game theory situation called the prisoners' dilemma, two individuals, both guilty of murder, are arrested and held separately by the police. The only evidence that will convict one individual is the testimony of the other. The police interrogators inform each prisoner of the "rules of the game": if neither gives evidence on the other, both will go free; if either or both cooperate, the punishment will be life imprisonment for any individual who cooperates; but if one cooperates and the other does not, the noncooperating individual will likely receive the death penalty.

In this dilemma, the prisoners would both be better off if they remained silent, since they would both go free. But silence would be fatal for one if the other prisoner cooperated. To minimize the danger, it is in the interest of both prisoners to cooperate and, in the process, convict each other of a crime, the punishment for which they could both avoid through mutual silence.

The use of fluorocarbons in aerosol products, analysts discovered, was a similar problem although without the same moral overtones. Virtually all competitors were using fluorocarbon packaging technology because it produced products with attributes consumers liked: ease of use and quality of spray. The nonaerosol methods of delivering hairsprays and antiperspirants were clearly cheaper, but if any one firm voluntarily shifted to these technologies and the others did not, consumers would presumably rush to the remaining fluorocarbon-propelled products, and the firm that switched to the low-cost technology would be worse off than if it continued using the high-cost packaging technique. Those consumers not switching to another brand might abandon the product altogether. Indeed, analysts had forecast that 40 percent of all hairspray users would prefer to cease using the product rather than switch to a nonaerosol version. Not surprisingly, in this market context most competitors pursued the high-cost packaging alternatives.[9]

If, however, all competitors simultaneously shifted to the alternative low-cost technologies, consumers would not have the option to switch and the industry's production costs might actually fall. Of course, consumers could still abandon the product altogether, but if the cost reductions were large enough and price changes less than fully compensating, even a smaller market might be a more profitable one.

Regulators, by banning the use of fluorocarbons, imposed the "cooperative" solution on the industry, thereby allowing industry to pursue the use of lower-cost production methods otherwise unattractive in an unregulated competitive setting. Whether the attendant loss of consumer convenience justified any reduction in production costs that may have resulted from this particular intervention is something that economists can argue, but there is little doubt that public action created an opportunity for management to reduce the costs of doing business in the cosmetics industry.

The fluorocarbon case is not unique. There are often instances in which the authority of government to enforce cooperative behavior can prove beneficial to an industry's interests. These beneficial effects do not require cost reduction, but they do require simultaneous action.

Earlier I referred to the safety devices installed on over-the-counter medicines after the Tylenol murders. There is no question that these packages are more costly than the alternatives. It is also clear that some individual competitors—notably, the makers of Tylenol—felt obliged to install these costly devices whether required by law or not in order to reclaim consumer confidence. As a practical matter, from a broader social perspective, the added safety of the new caps was not very great. Someone bent on this bizarre form of crime has numerous other consumer products to poison besides medicine. Nevertheless, it made some rather obvious marketing sense to take the precautionary action with regard to over-the-counter medication. In this instance, a rule requiring the use of similar packaging by all competitors meant that a potentially significant cost disadvantage for the competitor with a safer package would now be ameliorated by virtue of the fact that these higher costs were imposed on all producers. Moreover, a public requirement would signal to consumers an improvement in safety rather than a marketing gimmick by the makers of Tylenol. In this case, regulation increased production costs but probably eased industry concerns regarding the competitive advantage that would accrue to holdouts and helped protect the highly profitable over-the-counter drug market from erosion due to irrational as well as rational responses of concerned consumers.

A second example relates to fuel-efficient automobiles. As gasoline prices rose in the 1970s two things became clear: first, consumers would eventually shift to more fuel-efficient cars; but second, the demand for fuel economy in the short run was less than the demand in the long run because people do not really like to change their driving habits quickly. On the demand side of the auto market, therefore, while a long-run switch to fuel-efficient cars was inevitable, consumers were reluctant to switch quickly.[10]

On the supply side, there was similar hesitancy. The incremental costs of a wholesale conversion to substantially more fuel-efficient vehicles were very large, while more modest incremental improvements in the fuel efficiency of existing vehicles were much less costly. The combination of consumer hesitancy and low incremental costs for modest technological improvements could easily make a "go slow" strategy of conversion desirable to manufacturers.

Such a strategy might not be in the public interest, however, since fuel-inefficient cars increased the nation's vulnerability to political and economic manipulation by the international oil cartel.

One way to accelerate the transition to fuel-efficient autos was to impose rules that disciplined the transition and discouraged holdouts. This, of course, is one interpretation of the mandatory "corporate average fuel economy," or CAFE, standards that Congress imposed in December 1975. This was a clear effort to overcome any prisoners' dilemma confronting auto producers wishing to move the United States to a more fuel-efficient fleet.

Regulating Lead in Gasoline

The opportunity to use regulation to achieve an objective that many individual competitors would find otherwise attractive but elusive due to competitive market pressures arises with more frequency than we might expect. An almost classic case occurred early in the Reagan Administration when Anne Gorsuch, the ambitious new administrator of the EPA took seriously her presidential mandate to get her agency off the back of business.[11]

"Regulatory relief" for the business community had been a high initial priority of the new Reagan Administration. In his first months in office, President Reagan had issued an Executive Order requiring that a cost-benefit test be applied and met by all regulatory proposals. He also established a highly visible Task Force on Regulatory Relief, chaired by Vice President George Bush (a former oil industry executive), to identify existing regulations that could be relaxed.

The EPA quickly emerged as a major target, and on August 12, 1981, the Task Force directed the agency to examine the existing regulatory requirements aimed at phasing down the use of lead as a gasoline additive.

The EPA commissioned an economic study. In a November 30 memorandum to Administrator Gorsuch, Joel Schwartz of the Energy Economics branch reported that a relaxation of standards would save industry approximately $133 million. This saving, as the Iron Law tells us, would not be uniform across competitors. Rather, the large refiners who had already made major investments in alternative technologies would save approximately one-tenth of a cent per gallon while small refiners would save, on average, nine-tenths of a cent. For petroleum refiners this difference was substantial.

Understandably, environmentalists were not enthusiastic about any relaxation of these hard-won standards. The position of industry, however, was more complicated and less easy to understand. The National Petroleum Refiners Association (NPRA) supported relaxation—but with some reservations related to what they felt were "loopholes" in the rule the EPA had proposed. The loopholes concerned the ability of companies whose only business was the "blending" of gasoline to purchase inexpensive low-grade fuel, mix it with large amounts of lead to boost the octane, and undersell the refineries by as much as 5 cents per gallon.

If the EPA relaxed the rules on lead, these blenders would be able to continue to exploit this advantage in a marketplace in which, in the previous year, about forty domestic petroleum refineries had closed.

A similar concern related to importers of gasoline who were not subject to the same rules that faced domestic refiners. Thus, while the NPRA apparently supported a relaxation of the standards, the nature of their objections suggested that the existing rules were not only tolerable but perhaps even desirable in that they might help reduce the glut in overall refining supply and the competitive threat of imported gasoline.

Some of the larger producers, such as Mobil and Exxon, were actively against the relaxation, arguing that the advantage to their competitors was especially unfair given their own prior commitments of capital to comply with the standards.

With environmentalists and the medical community favoring tougher standards and many in industry opposing relaxation of the rules, the EPA withdrew its proposal. Instead, in what was seen as a dramatic change in policy, the EPA made it known on July 30, 1982, that it would actually tighten the limits on lead additives in gasoline.

At the outset of this policy deliberation, it had seemed logical for Anne Gorsuch to loosen these requirements. After all, such an action would presumably be met with favor by the industrial interests that had supported the Reagan candidacy.

Not so. Ms. Gorsuch had apparently failed to appreciate fully the competitive effects of her proposed regulatory actions. At the time of her proposal to reduce standards, the petroleum-refining industry was experiencing a glut in supply and attendant downward price pressures. A relaxation of standards would have expanded the already excess available supply of gasoline-refining capacity and added to these downward price pressures. In other words, standard relaxation would not only result in a dirtier environment, but it could cost the regulated industry profits as well. Obviously, this was a politically unattractive combination. The Iron Law, of course, indicated that some competitors would win with this regulation, but apparently the political beneficiaries were relatively few in number.

What the EPA regulators had discovered was that the business interest in any particular regulatory action can only be determined after an examination of the competitive dynamics set in motion by public policy. In this instance, an industry already suffering from excess capacity was unlikely to benefit from actions that would add to this surplus. The EPA had almost missed an important opportunity to take advantage of these competitive and political realities to advance its own program's interests.

It is also worth noting that two years after this policy reversal, the EPA once again tightened the standards for leaded gasoline.[12]

The Importance of Joint Action

The ban of fluorocarbons, which helped reduce costs by eliminating the most expensive packaging technology from consideration, is not unlike the establishment of rules of contract or some other law controlling business behavior. By compelling joint action—"use no fluorocarbons" or "obey contractual commitments"—government action can reduce the cost of doing business.

Having observed that public actions can sometimes decrease the costs of doing business, it would be tempting to estimate the levels of these cost reductions nationwide and subtract them from Murray Weidenbaum's $141 billion to show the "true net cost" of regulation to U.S. business. Such a figure could be terribly misleading, however, in any discussion of the competitive effects of government policy. It might actually reveal that the true net cost of government regulation was negative; after all, among the biggest obstacles to economic growth one typically sees in less developed nations is the absence of viable rules of business conduct. Economies do not thrive in the presence of corruption, lack of rules, and the like.[13]

While a negative "true net cost" figure would be reassuring evidence of the benefits of good government, it would be incorrect to conclude from a such a figure that the competitive consequences for individual enterprises of government action were either inconsequential or even necessarily positive. Any discussion of the competitive effects of government policy must recognize that it is the *differences* in costs among competitors—whether cost increases or decreases—that determine the ultimate consequences for an individual competitor's bottom line.

Moreover, even from a broader social perspective, the finding of a negative "true net cost" of government intervention could be misleading. Such a conclusion might mask the fact that many programs of government intervention are excessively costly and socially unproductive. It would also mask the fact that the critical consequences of governmental actions are not always measured in costs.

While it is interesting to note that government actions can both increase and decrease costs, from a competitive perspective, whether costs rise or fall *in the aggregate* is largely—although not entirely—irrelevant. Obviously, if costs increase so much as to endanger the continued existence of an industry—as in the case of water pollution controls and the metal finishing industry—then aggregate costs matter a great deal.[14] But typically we are not talking about putting an industry out of business; rather we are talking about the creation of cost differentials among competitors with attendant implications for market share, profitability, and business risk. In this setting, higher costs are not always bad.

The auto industry is a good case in point. Given the choice between cheap or expensive gasoline, there is no doubt that automakers' interests are better served by low gasoline prices. A policy of keeping the price of gasoline low by government fiat, however, does not make gasoline cheap; it merely hides its true cost to the consumer for the temporary period in which regulations are in place. Given the resulting regulatory uncertainty and the confusing market signals that consumers conveyed to auto manufacturers when they did face artificially low gasoline prices in the 1970s, the regulators' efforts to reduce the costs of driving may have done the industry no favor. In contrast, fuel-economy standards, to the extent that they helped the industry overcome the competitive incentives to go slow on fuel-economy improvement, may have been competitively advantageous, even though they undoubtedly added to the cost of auto manufacturing.[15]

Any simple accounting of the "costs of regulation" to the consumer would show gasoline price controls lowering costs and fuel-economy requirements raising them. Arithmetically this would be correct. Such arithmetic, however, could yield poor public policy and counterproductive competitive consequences, since both public policy interests and competitive business interests were better served by efficient, market-determined gasoline prices. Thus not only is it difficult to measure the aggregate costs of government intervention, but it may be misleading or unhelpful to do so if the differential impacts among firms and the net benefit to society of public action are not simultaneously taken into account.

The Importance of Relative Costs

In most cases, the key competitive effects of government policy are traceable to changes in *relative* costs. A competitor who experiences a small cost increase due to public action but whose competitors experience large cost increases is likely to feel far better about his competitive position than someone whose firm experiences small decreases in costs at the same time competitors' costs drop significantly.

The importance of relative cost changes among competitors —whether increases or decreases—cannot be overstressed. To illustrate this point, consider the common case in which government actions increase costs.

In any industry there are always low-cost producers and high-cost producers, irrespective of the actions of government. Similarly, in the face of any given government policy, there are firms for which the costs of compliance are high, firms for which the costs are low, and firms for which the costs are in between.

As a case in point, consider how water pollution control costs varied among competitors in the tissue paper manufacturing industry. One low-cost plant in this industry was able to comply with environmental requirements at an estimated average total cost of $1.52 per ton of output, while the average competitor had to spend $6.74 per ton. The costs were higher for the average facility because of less up-to-date facilities and production technologies. At the extreme, one facility had to spend $21.04 per ton of product to comply with the EPA's water requirements.[16]

The tissue paper industry is not unique in having widely varying costs of regulatory compliance; such variations are observable over and over again in other industrial settings. Typically, firms with high compliance costs have costs well above those of their low-cost competitors. Even the more than ten-to-one ratio experienced in the tissue industry is not unique. Regulatory compliance costs for high-cost firms were found to be ten to twenty times those of their low-cost competitors in other cases as well. In a larger study of other sectors of the paper industry, for example, investigators at the National Bureau of Economic Research estimated that low-cost competitors could meet federal water pollution control requirements for an incremental cost of $1.21 per ton. High-cost producers, in contrast, faced costs in excess of $69.40 per ton of the same product.[17]

In the tissue industry case just cited the high-cost manufacturer is also a small producer. Given scale economies in regulatory compliance, this, too, is an accurate depiction of many real-world competitive conditions.

Of course, the tissue paper industry includes a large number of competitors. And each of them would also experience a unique cost to comply with water pollution control requirements. These differences stem from differences in technology, scale, geographic location, and local circumstance. For example, some facilities in this industry have the misfortune of being sited on bedrock, which makes the cost of excavating holding ponds and lagoons very high.

The critical reality illustrated by this example is that not all competitors face the same cost to comply with any given regulatory requirement. This simple fact is at the heart of the Iron Law of Public Policy: while governmental action may increase the costs of doing business, these cost increases are not the same for all competitors. Just as differential wage costs, raw material costs, or capital costs can be the source of competitive advantage and disadvantage, differential costs of regulatory compliance can—and do—affect the competitiveness of individual firms.

These differential compliance costs reveal a good deal about the competitive effects of government action, especially when we consider another basic principle of economics. Fundamental principles of competitive markets tell us that production cost changes will ultimately show up in price changes. That is not to say that *all* increases or decreases in costs of production can be passed through to the consumer, but it does say that when costs change, changes in price are likely to follow. In practice, of course, the magnitude of any price change the marketplace will sustain depends on a variety of competitive factors, but in any case the resulting price change is the same for all competitors. After all, there is no reason for consumers to pay more because a product is manufactured in a plant with high production costs. Similarly, low-cost competitors are not obligated to share their efficiency with their customers.

Since the price effects of regulation are essentially the same for all producers, but cost effects differ, public actions necessarily affect firms differently. All firms with cost increases less than the price increase actually see their profits *increase* with government intervention. Those firms with cost increases above the level of sustainable price increases experience losses. Similarly, if government action drives down costs, but prices fall still more, an individual competitor suffers a reduction in profit. All of this, of course, is the Iron Law of Public Policy at work: so long as the cost changes induced by governmental action vary among competitors but price changes are uniform, there will always be winners and losers within industry.

The aggregate impact on the industry is the sum of the gains and losses to individual competitors. It is easy to see that from the perspective of individual firms, the industry aggregate is a relatively "uninteresting" statistic. Whether the sum is large or small, the impact on an individual firm can be great.

Consider the EPA's estimates of the cost and price effects of water pollution control policies. According to these estimates, the pulp and paper industry as a whole was forecast to lose profits—technically called "lost contributions to capital" by the EPA—of $36 million per year. This loss, however, was by no means shared uniformly across the industry. The results for individual sectors varied dramatically.[18]

In fact, for eight of the fourteen product segments for which the EPA made estimates, profits were actually forecast to increase with regulation. Thus the $36 million net loss was the sum of a $101 million loss for the losing segments and a $65 million gain for the winning segments.

But even product sector aggregation masks the true winners and losers. For example, the "special industrial papers" product category was forecast to earn $5 million more annually due to pollution control–induced price increases of $5.80 per ton. The plants in this industrial category with the lowest pollution control costs were expected to see costs rise by only $2.40 per ton, for a clear gain. At the other extreme, however, were competitors with cost increases of $8.30 per ton. On average, price increases were forecast to exceed costs, but for individual firms there were still gains and losses.

For another category of paperboard manufacturers, the aggregate losses were substantial. Many competitors were forecast to experience cost increases in excess of $3 to $5 per ton but price increases of only 50 cents. Even in this product group, however, some competitors had cost increases of 40 cents and were expected to see their profits increase with pollution abatement.

Basically, two factors determine the extent of these gains and losses: the cost increases sustained by individual competitors and the extent of any price changes triggered by public policy. Both of these factors are subject to direct managerial and political control through various means.

Consider first the costs of individual competitors. Public authorities have numerous ways to alter these costs and hence the competitive consequences of public action. For example, they can "subcategorize" an industry into different segments and impose different rules for different segments. By imposing rules that are less costly on those facilities which would otherwise be high-cost compliers, they can sharply reduce the competitive disadvantage of those firms. This practice is allowed for explicitly in the 1972 Clean Water Act, for example.[19]

On the other hand, authorities can increase the costs for those producers who would otherwise experience low costs by imposing more stringent rules on them. Since it is often cheaper to install compliance equipment in new facilities than in existing ones, regulators often achieve this effect with stringent "new source performance" requirements that apply only to new facilities. Such standards are commonplace in the present structure of U.S. regulation.

Still another way to dramatically influence the costs of individual competitors is through the careful choice of regulatory form—one obvious choice involves the use of nationally uniform versus regionally variable regulatory requirements.

For example, federal water pollution control regulations that took effect in 1977 applied the same regulatory standard to all competitors in an industry subcategory.[20] This did not yield uniform costs, of course, because even the same rule imposed throughout the nation yields different costs for different firms for reasons of scale, geography, age, and so forth. However, the alternative rule, which would have varied regulatory requirements regionally to reflect the water quality requirements of the areas in which firms were located, would have created substantially more variation in costs among competitors. Indeed, given such a rule, some producers would have had zero costs since the waters into which they discharged their effluent already met the EPA's goals for water quality; and many of the high-cost firms would have had still higher costs, because some water bodies need so much improvement.[21]

Note that in the case where cleanup varies with water quality, treatment would occur only if justified by the environmental benefits. Needless to say, this was the policy economists tended to prefer. Despite the implications for overall economic efficiency, such a policy would have created some very large winners and similarly large losers within the industrial sector. These gains and losses were significantly reduced, although far from eliminated, by the adoption of the uniform national standard.

Industry tended to support the uniform approach, perhaps reflecting the general hesitancy of U.S. managements to enthusiastically endorse activities that challenge the market share status quo. In any case, Congress chose the uniform rule and not only reduced industry's objection to regulation, but elicited its active support. The result was a very stringent water pollution control law that violated strict principles of economic efficiency but that otherwise satisfied political criteria for an acceptable policy in a competitive market setting.

In addition to the differences in costs of regulatory compliance among competitors, the other critical determinant of the competitive effects of governmental action is the level of any price change triggered by public policy. There are various ways government authorities can manipulate this price increase. The results of this manipulation can profoundly affect the competitive consequences for individual firms.

It is a basic principle of supply and demand that prices are set to reflect the costs of the marginal producer in an industry—not the highest-cost producer, not the lowest-cost firm, but that last or "marginal" producer that can barely justify production at a price consumers are willing to pay. While this is a basic principle of economics, it is not necessarily a widely shared notion. After all, one's instinctive reaction is that prices are set by the lowest-cost producers. But a moment's consideration indicates why this is not the case. If lowest-cost producers are able to sell all of their available output, they will have a strong inclination to raise prices. As they do so, other competitors will find it profitable to enter the market. They will be content to raise prices as well so long as they too can sell their output. The process will stop when a firm no longer finds customers willing to bear the burden of higher prices. This "marginal" producer will have a clear incentive to set prices just at a level to cover variable costs and thus maximize total market share and profitability. This process leads us to conclude that prices are set in competitive markets by the costs of the marginal producer.

The importance of this observation lies in the fact that government policy makers, by manipulating the regulatory compliance costs of the marginal producer, can effectively manipulate price. The capacity to manage compliance costs, therefore, not only determines the extent to which costs vary among competitors due to public action but also determines the price effects of governmental action. The net result of these cost and price impacts determines whether an individual competitor ends up a winner or a loser.[22]

It is tempting to think that firms with low production costs also have low compliance costs and high-cost manufacturers have high compliance costs. If this were the case, the industry's marginal producers would be the ones to receive the largest cost increases due to government intervention. Because such cost increases determine price increases in competitive markets, the result would likely be substantial price increases. Because such price increases would equal the cost increases actually experienced by those firms with the highest costs, they would be, by definition, higher than the cost increases experienced by other, lower-cost manufacturers.

There is nothing to guarantee, however, that compliance costs are highest for an industry's marginal producers or are otherwise correlated with production costs. Indeed, for political reasons one might expect just the opposite to be the case. Since the general public sees price increases but not cost increases, it would make a good deal of political sense to minimize price impacts by constructing rules so that high-cost producers have relatively low compliance costs—say through the subcategorization of industry. Through this means, the sustainable price increase in the marketplace would be relatively low. Indeed, this is the pattern that was actually observed in the paper industry.[23] In eight of sixteen product categories in the paper industry, the high-cost producers experienced low regulatory compliance costs.

Differential Costs Matter

Once we recognize that public actions affect costs differentially but prices uniformly, there is no avoiding the Iron Law of Public Policy and its consequences:

1. By virtue of differential cost impacts, all governmental actions create winners and losers in the competitive marketplace, whether or not the aggregate impact is beneficial or detrimental to an industry's interests.
2. Private firms can be expected to exercise their political and economic strength to jockey for the positions of winners.
3. Regulators and elected decision makers, sensitive to the inherently (and legitimately) political nature of these gains and losses, will likely try to "manage" these impacts for both their own political and broader public purposes through the various means available to them.

If we are to understand the competitive effects of public actions, we must understand the conjunction of these economic and political forces and the consequent implications for the actions of various actors in this process. Indeed, this conjunction of political and economic forces confronts public policy makers with a number of extremely difficult decisions.

Consider the possibility of effluent fees for pollution control. The economists' favorite solution to a wide variety of public policy problems is to let market forces resolve them by creating economic incentives. This approach has several obvious advantages, most notably the efficiency of decentralized, profit-maximizing decisions. The economists' plan is to establish a charge —an effluent fee—for all discharges into the environment. Despite the theoretical attractiveness of such fees from the standpoint of economic efficiency, they play a negligible role in U.S. environmental policy. An examination of their implications for individual competitors helps explain why.

When an effluent fee is imposed on industry, firms with compliance costs less than the fee will tend to clean up pollution rather than pay the fee, since cleanup is cheaper. In contrast, high-cost compliers will prefer to pay the fee. The fee, in other words, places a cap on compliance costs. This is, of course, the attractiveness of the fee from a social perspective because it avoids situations where excessively high costs are incurred to achieve a particular improvement in environmental quality.

While the fee is attractive from a social perspective, it can look less attractive from the perspective of individual competitors because a fee places a cap on some competitors' costs, but all competitors' prices increase.

Consider the impact of the effluent fee from the perspective of low-cost producers. It does not place any effective cap on their costs because they can more cheaply clean up the pollution than pay the fee. With or without the fee, they spend the same amount for pollution cleanup. In contrast, the price increases that the industry will experience are now capped by the fee. Because their costs do not fall but their revenues may well decline, there is little incentive to support the fee.

Now consider the impact on high-cost producers. In the absence of the fee, compliance costs were high, but competitive pressures forced price increases that largely offset these costs. The negative impact of pollution control to these producers came not from reduced profit margins—since price increases offset cost increases—but from reduced sales attributable to higher prices. A cap on costs associated with an effluent fee lowers costs but also lowers prices. Again, the net impact on margins is minimal. There is, of course, benefit from the higher sales volumes associated with lower prices, but if the high-cost producer is already operating at close to zero profit, there may be little *absolute* profit for these producers to gain from the volume increase a fee alternative would yield. With one group within industry losing and the other group gaining very little, it is not surprising that there is little support from industry for the fee.

In fact, since the empirical evidence suggests that a substantial portion of industry capacity—in several studies, up to 80 percent—counts itself among the winners due to environmental controls, the result is a very large number of competitors who are likely to lose with effluent fees but small numbers of producers who gain.[24]

An arithmetic example illustrates the point. Suppose an industry is heavily burdened by the costs of a stringent pollution control program, but the industry's marginal competitors are particularly hard hit. To be specific, let us suppose the low-cost competitor experiences cost increases of $1 per unit output but the marginal competitors experience cost increases of $2. In the absence of policy intervention, prices will rise due to market forces by an amount equal to the costs of the marginal producers, or $2.

Now suppose we establish a program of tax credits for pollution control that reduces the effective cost of pollution control by 50 percent. The marginal competitors experience only a $1 cost increase—hence prices rise by only $1. The average producer also sees costs reduced by 50 percent, or a total of 50 cents. On balance, the cost-reducing tax policy lowered price more than cost for the low-cost or "inframarginal" producers and hence *reduced* their profits. Although the industry's marginal producers benefited from the general demand stimulus created by the policy-induced cost decrease, aggregate profits could actually decline under this presumably "pro-industry" tax policy.

While the real world is not quite so tidy as this example suggests, the existence of differential costs among competitors can set in motion a sometimes counterintuitive set of political forces—forces that help explain widespread industrial opposition to many of the so-called market solutions to public policy problems one might otherwise expect business to champion.

When these differential costs are taken into account, it is not surprising to see low-cost automobile manufacturers like

Honda actively support the mandatory installation of passive restraints in automobiles; or high-quality, fuel-efficient appliance manufacturers like Amana support mandatory energy-efficiency standards. Both policies would increase the costs of production in these two industries—but with likely beneficial impacts on both firms.

Some of the most interesting political battles take place when competing firms each possess a competitive advantage that they then seek to impose on the competition as a requirement of public policy. In the debates over auto emissions standards, for example, General Motors' expertise in catalytic converters and Chrysler's expertise in electronics were presumably important determinants of their respective positions on the important issue of exhaust emissions controls.

In a more recent case, several chain-saw manufacturers have battled over the establishment of safety standards by the Consumer Products Safety Commission (CPSC) to prevent "kickback."[25] Kickback is the sudden and potentially violent rearward and/or upward movement of the chain guide bar that can result from interference with the chain's movement. While many conditions can cause kickback, most accidents apparently result from contact between the chain bar and a log or tree limb while the chain is moving. The resulting injuries can be severe if the moving chain hits the chest, throat, or face of the operator. The CPSC estimated that in 1978, 23 percent of the 77,000 chain-saw–related injuries were caused by kickback.

The battle over standards was not so much over whether government should regulate chain-saw safety but over which manufacturer's solution to the kickback problem should be codified in law. There are two basic approaches to reducing kickback hazards. One is to reduce the possibility of kickback with a guard or an antikickback chain. The Homelite Company, for example, fitted its saw with nose guards. The Beaird-Poulan Company installed antikickback chains.

The second solution is a chain brake that allows kickback to occur but stops the saw before it can hit the operator. This is accomplished with a lever in front of the operator's hand that engages as the saw rotates toward the operator. McCulloch installed chain brakes on all its models, while Beaird-Poulan and Homelite made them optional on a few models. Chain brakes were quite expensive at an estimated cost of $19.70 per saw versus $1 to $2 for the other devices. In addition, chain brakes had to be designed into the saws and could not be simply added later, unlike nose guards and antikickback chains.

In 1977 Homelite had a 22 to 25 percent market share (in unit sales), Beaird-Poulan had a 20 to 23 percent market share, and McCulloch had a 19 to 21 percent market share. There was no clear market leader and the market was expanding rapidly. Strategically, Homelite emphasized low price while McCulloch emphasized quality and safety.

When the CPSC proposed a mandatory standard, Homelite helped organize the Chain Saw Manufacturers Association (CSMA) to deal with regulation. McCulloch and others joined. In June 1978 the CPSC authorized the CSMA to develop a voluntary industry standard. By January 1980 the CMSA had made little progress due largely to differences among its members. The apparent reason that the CMSA could not develop a standard on its own was that the competitive interests of its members differed so greatly. McCulloch, not surprisingly and consistent with its marketing strategy, advocated a quick and strong regulation requiring chain brakes; Homelite, consistent with its marketing approach, wished to continue using nose guards. The voluntary efforts were deadlocked by understandable efforts of individual competitors to advocate policies that each felt met both consumer and competitive interests.

In September 1980 the CPSC published notice that it would develop its own mandatory standard.

The Policy Maker's Dilemma

As the preceding discussion of policy-induced cost changes has shown, it is impossible for policy makers to implement programs that change the cost of doing business without creating winners and losers *within* the affected industry.

Because the term "winners and losers" is frequently employed in the industrial policy debate, it is important to stress that we have been discussing *intra*-industry competitive effects. Typically, when the industrial policy debate considers winners and losers, *industries* selected for favorable treatment are considered "winners" and those chosen for a policy of benign neglect are considered "losers." Our discussion indicates that there will also be winners and losers *within* both the favored and disadvantaged sectors, with consequent political implications.

Thus, even a policy maker who champions a public policy that will reduce the cost of doing business will not be met with unanimous approval from the business sector. There will be great concern among the inevitable losers, for example, for the pattern of any cost reduction that might occur among competitors in an industry, and less general enthusiasm for the prospects of cost reduction than might otherwise be expected.

In the examples just cited, the interests of industry as a whole and certainly the interests of individual competitors were not necessarily advanced by the cost-reducing efforts of policy makers. It is important to stress that this was not due to specific attributes of the examples but is rather a general conclusion. Whenever an industry's marginal competitors are most adversely affected by government action, there is likely to be political pressure to adopt policies that reduce costs. Given that marginal facilities are often small and old, and often represent an important source of local employment, the political desire to avoid costly economic and social disruption is understandable.

This discussion, of course, highlights the fact that economic policy is a public initiative precisely because it is designed to achieve the public interests that might well be served by lower costs, lower prices, less painful disruption of marginal competitors, and the like. There is no doubt, however, that policy makers, when confronting the divergence of public interests and private competitive interests, will see the conflict as posing a dilemma. Whether the dilemma will be resolved to the public's interest remains to be seen.

Chapter 4

Government and the

Cost Structure of Firms

The last chapter examined the considerable impact of government policy on the overall cost of doing business. The discussion showed that public actions typically affect the production costs of individual competitors differently. These differences in the levels of compliance costs, like any other cost differentials businesses experience, could be an important source of competitive effects. This chapter also considers the impact of government on the cost of doing business, but focuses not on the level but on the composition or "structure" of these costs. The impact of government policy on the cost structure of doing business often can have far more serious consequences for competing firms than do impacts of government policy on the overall level of production costs.

The Fixed-Cost Problem

An example illustrates the point. In its formulation of effluent guidelines for the pulp and paper industry, the Environmental Protection Agency (EPA) set out to identify the lowest-cost methods of regulatory compliance. As one might expect, this exercise required scrutiny of a large number of technological alternatives for water pollution control and fundamental process change. Naturally, these alternatives varied in what economists call "factor intensities": some involved high capital costs but promised low operating costs; others required less capital but necessitated the use of more chemicals and other raw materials on an ongoing basis; still others had relatively high labor costs, and so forth.

To identify the so-called lowest-cost option, the EPA created "annualized equivalents" of all capital and other fixed costs and added them to the recurring operating and maintenance costs of the different technologies. From the resulting list the lowest-cost methods were then identified. For water pollution control, these lowest-cost options typically involved some form of biological waste treatment. The science of biological waste treatment is not important to us. Suffice it to observe that a residential septic system is one common form of biological waste treatment. The point critical to this discussion is that biological waste treatment is capital intensive—as with your home septic system, there are substantial initial costs but relatively low variable costs and minimal recurring expenses once a facility is operating.

This fixed-cost characteristic has significant competitive implications that go well beyond the fact that water pollution control increases the cost of manufacturing pulp and paper products. For one thing, it increases the "operating leverage" of paper manufacturing firms. Operating leverage refers to the fact that any fixed-cost enterprise must operate at some minimum level of capacity utilization to break even. The higher the break-even utilization rate, the higher the operating leverage of the enterprise. Water pollution controls, by increasing the fixed costs of paper production, increase the minimum level of capacity that firms have to utilize in order to operate profitably. Any increase in operating leverage increases a competitor's vulnerability to downturns in the business cycle, among other effects. The importance of this point lies in the fact that a low-cost technology can be unattractive once the issue of cost structure is considered explicitly. Indeed, if a company's management was particularly concerned about the risks of a cyclical decline in economic activity, it would not commit itself to a high fixed-cost investment, despite analysis of the type employed by the EPA showing that high fixed-cost facilities had the lowest total costs.

The Cost of Capital

Not only do capital-intensive pollution control technologies directly increase the fixed costs of doing business, but they increase these fixed costs indirectly by adding to the cost of acquiring capital. First, they increase the total demand for funds and thereby contribute to higher borrowing charges. This effect is a straightforward consequence of the fact that the price of any commodity—in this case, money—rises when the demand for it increases. These higher capital charges, of course, apply not only to the capital required for investments in regulatory compliance but to the firm's entire borrowing needs.

The impact on an individual firm can be dramatic. An electric utility, for example, may find that pollution control expenditures require it to go to the capital markets to borrow $50 million. For many large utilities these days this is a relatively small sum of money. The added interest costs might lower the firm's interest coverage ratio or otherwise affect investor's expectations about the firm's long-run financial condition. An increase in the cost of capital to this company of twenty-five basis points—one-quarter of one percent—might not be unreasonable. But if this firm also had several billions of dollars of additional debt outstanding and some of it coming due, these added basis points would be tacked on to the refinancing charges for the other loans. The absolute increase in fixed capital costs could be several times greater than what one would predict by looking only at the direct increase in fixed costs associated with the pollution control investments.

As if this demand effect is not enough, there is also a risk effect. Because capital-intensive technologies increase operating leverage they also increase the risk inherent in doing business. As with any other increase in risk, potential investors respond by raising the return they require to commit their funds to the enterprise.

Semi-Fixed Costs

And the impact of higher fixed costs does not end there. In addition to increasing capital charges, high fixed-cost compliance technologies like biological treatment technologies in the paper industry also increase the semifixed costs of doing business on an ongoing basis. While it is technically inelegant to express it this way, the essence of a biological treatment system is the living biota—"bugs"—that eat the manufacturing plant's pollution. If the treatment system is to remain functional, these living organisms must be fed whether or not the facility is producing.

The significance of this impact was brought home to me during a public hearing on effluent controls that occurred a decade ago during the "sugar crisis"—a time when sugar prices had increased five- to tenfold in a matter of months. A local paper manufacturing plant manager, speaking of his concern for the EPA's choice of so-called low-cost technology, pointed out that he was compelled to "feed" his waste treatment system sugar during a plant shutdown. Since his was a marginally competitive facility to begin with, this added fixed cost was a serious drain on his firm's already limited cash flow.

By increasing the fixed and semifixed costs of doing business, public actions can dramatically affect short-term competitive conditions.

Production Strategy

The nature of these impacts varies among firms, depending on the strategies they use to compete in the marketplace. Thus students of production management frequently make the distinction between so-called level and chase production strategies. In level production strategies, management attempts to minimize the cost of manufacturing by reducing fluctuations in production levels. During down markets, this requires the manufacture of goods for either a finished product or a parts inventory; during up markets, sales are made from this inventory. Since inventories serve as a buffer between supply and demand, the company typically must manufacture its product to predetermined specifications and not alter them to satisfy particular customer desires. Firms with this strategy often compete more on the basis of price than on the basis of service, quality, or variety. The extreme application of this strategy, of course, was Henry Ford's "any color so long as it's black" marketing policy.

In contrast, some firms consciously choose chase production strategies. Instead of building a large finished product inventory, they adjust output to meet current levels of demand—that is, they "chase" demand. Because these firms can adapt to the needs of the marketplace on short order but do so at higher cost, they often emphasize quality and service in their marketing. Furniture manufacturers, in an attempt to respond to widely varying customer preferences for upholstery fabric and design, typically employ such a strategy, which leads to the customary two- or three-month delay in receiving new furniture. While firms that follow this strategy have lower inventory holding costs, they have higher overall production costs because customization is an inherently costly activity.

Typically, firms employ level production strategies because they confront high operating leverage; that is, a substantial average unit cost advantage comes from a sustained high level of capacity utilization. Firms employing chase strategies, in contrast, seek to avoid operating leverage because high fixed costs are very unattractive in slack markets when a chase strategy requires management to idle facilities. Public policies that increase operating leverage by increasing the fixed costs of doing business inadvertently penalize those producers committed to chase production strategies, for they make the penalty for such strategies larger than they might be otherwise.

This impact is by no means inconsequential. It can represent an especially important penalty today for many U.S. manufacturers who must compete with low-cost offshore producers. With labor costs relatively high in the United States, it is often difficult for domestic producers to pursue successfully competitive strategies based strictly on low production costs.

At the same time competitive strategies not based on low costs depend for success on the ability to satisfy customers' needs for variety, specialization, service, and so forth, if not price. Often these nonprice strategies involve the pursuit of chase production strategies in which competitors use a flexible production capacity to meet their customers' special needs— and thus merit a premium price.

Government policies that increase operating leverage and encourage level production strategies work against these more flexible strategies at the very same time they make strategies based on low product costs more difficult to pursue. It is a double whammy for U.S. industry: regulations are imposed on U.S. firms that are not necessarily imposed on their foreign competitors. By itself, this makes a low-cost strategy less feasible for U.S. producers. But to minimize this cost penalty, the regulations are often imposed in such a manner that they further penalize those competitive strategies that are not low-cost based. Thus we face the irony that as policy makers try to lower the total costs of government regulation—by requiring biological waste treatment, for example—they often further inhibit non-cost-based strategies by increasing operating leverage and the semifixed costs of production.

This competitive bias against chase production strategies is particularly relevant to the nation's so-called smokestack industries. These basic manufacturing industries often face stiff

international competition from low-cost, high-volume producers that pursue level production strategies aggressively. Indeed,
foreign producers often pursue such strategies as a matter of
public policy aimed at maintaining high levels of employment
in their countries. One way for U.S. producers to combat such
cost-based competition in serving American markets is to emphasize the service, quality, and product variety that their offshore competitors cannot deliver. The inadvertent bias of U.S.
regulatory policy against such "chase" strategies can undercut
the efforts of domestic firms to compete effectively.

An example is the steel industry. The capital costs associated
with pollution control investments alone can add several percentage points to the cost of a new steel mill in the United
States.[1] Given both high labor costs and stringent environmental regulation, it is not surprising that no new large, integrated
steel mill has been built in the United States since Bethlehem's
Burns Harbor facility was opened in Indiana in 1960. How
could such facilities possibly compete with international suppliers who aggressively operate at high rates of capacity utilization in both good times and bad times? These foreign firms can
justify the requisite price cutting in slack markets either on the
basis of their high operating leverage or on the dictates of their
own domestic government policies. In either case, it is especially
difficult for U.S. producers to compete successfully with these
firms strictly on the basis of price.

Yet there are many profitable domestic steelmakers, and new
facilities are being opened frequently. These new facilities,
however, are not large-scale, integrated production operations
that compete strictly on the basis of cost; they are small, nonin-
tegrated facilities—so-called minimills—that compete on the
basis of service and flexibility of response to their customers'
needs as much as price. These new facilities typify the methods
used by firms to succeed when they are not necessarily low-cost
producers: locate close to markets, have low fixed costs and
short lead times, provide high-quality service, and be responsive to customers' needs.

Minimills can successfully pursue this strategy in large part because the electric furnace technology many of them employ confronts relatively few regulatory obstacles. Pollution control costs, for example, are incurred indirectly in the form of high electricity rates—rates, by the way, that are paid largely on a variable-cost and not a fixed-cost basis.

Cost Structure Is a Matter of Policy

Policy makers, it must be stressed, often have the discretion to choose between the imposition of fixed versus variable regulatory compliance costs. Private sector decision makers, in contrast, do not possess the same flexibility. Two obvious cases come to mind. The first involves effluent charges for pollution control versus mandatory technological solutions. An effluent fee is a variable cost of doing business; if a firm is not bothered by fixed costs, it can turn this variable cost into a fixed cost by installing capital-intensive technologies that minimize effluent and, consequently, variable fees. In contrast, when technological requirements are imposed, firms often lack the discretion to turn them into variable costs.*

The second example involves competition between trucks and trains. Railroads, by virtue of their ownership of track and right-of-way, face high fixed costs of doing business. Trucking companies, in contrast, do not incur the fixed costs of the nation's highways, but pay for them on a variable or semifixed basis through license fees and fuel taxes. There is considerable public debate as to whether trucks pay their full share of the nation's highways through these fees.[3] There is less discussion of the cost structure issue, however.

Even if trucks do pay their full share, they do so on a vari-

---

*In theory, this is not true. It is conceptually possible for a firm to lease a fixed-cost effluent treatment facility, where the provisions of the lease allow payments to vary with production levels. In practice, this is not done because of the various rules of taxation and ownership associated with leasing capital assets that are an integral part of a production facility.[2]

able-cost basis. By itself, this reduces their business risk relative to railroads. But even more important than this reduction in risk is the fact that the inclusion of the fixed costs of the highway as a variable cost of the trucking firm decreases the competitive pressure to price unprofitably in the short run. Since even the most aggressive competitor will not price below variable costs, the inclusion of fixed highway charges as variable fees helps reduce cutthroat competition in the trucking industry. Similar restraints are lacking in railroads, and the pressure to price at (low) marginal costs can be intense, especially during otherwise slack markets. From time to time, there have been proposals to nationalize the railroad rights-of-way and charge the cost of using them back to the railroads on a variable-cost basis. While some advocates of such a policy have seen it as a convenient way to subsidize the railroad industry, others have seen its attraction in the shift to a variable-cost structure.

Economies of Scale

When fixed costs are increased, there are often significant economies of scale. Thus public actions can affect the minimum scale for efficient operation with associated competitive impacts. The metal finishing industry represents an extreme illustration of the point.[4] Water pollution controls in this industry are extremely costly, first, because the effluent is inherently dirty and difficult to clean up, but also because the typical operator is very small. Indeed, these firms are so small that no one is quite sure just how many there are. The National Commission on Water Quality estimated that water pollution controls, by increasing the cost of metal finishing services, would reduce demand and thus drive some operators out of business. Far more important, however, the commission's analysts noted that pollution control could increase the minimum efficient scale of the typical metal finisher by a factor of five. That is, an industry with perhaps 70,000 individual firms prior to regulation might ultimately be able to support no more than about 14,000 operators after regulations were imposed even if demand were totally unaffected by higher prices.

Consider the ripple effects of such a situation. Customers of metal finishing firms would experience a dramatic shift in supplier relationships with the attendant costs of such disruption. More important, literally thousands of individual suppliers must decide whether to commit themselves to so substantial an increase in scale. How likely are 70,000 individual entrepreneurs to make decisions that, in the aggregate, yield neither excess nor deficient capacity in the short run? Ultimately, of course, these imbalances would be worked out, but in the short run, the risks of doing business increase more than one might expect from the increase in pollution control costs alone.

Labor Costs

Not all increases in fixed costs are associated with higher capital charges. General Motors, for example, estimates that it has a permanent staff of 22,000 full-time employees to deal with regulations at all government levels.[5] This is approximately 5 percent of the firm's total employment and, while not a fixed capital expense, is a relatively fixed overhead cost of substantial magnitude.

Nor, for that matter, do regulations always affect labor costs by increasing overhead expenses. The consequences of public actions for cost structure can occur without any great increase in production costs. For example, many states have introduced legislation requiring deposits on soft drink and beer containers as a means of reducing roadside litter. In those markets where deposits encourage the use of refillable bottles, total costs probably drop; in those markets where consumers so value the convenience of one-way containers as to continue purchasing them, costs probably rise. In both markets, however, the ratio of labor to total costs increases because the handling associated with the collection of containers and the return of deposits is a labor-intensive activity.

This shift to more labor-intensive production has major competitive implications. With labor costs relatively more important, the attractiveness of large-scale, centralized brewing and bottling operations decreases. This detracts from the competitive advantage of the large-scale, well-capitalized competitor.

In contrast, the increased importance of labor costs magnifies the competitive significance of efficient local operations management and labor cost control. Typically the local owner-operator of the bottling facility is benefited while firms with skills in advertising and access to capital but with weaker local management control are at a relative disadvantage. In the soft-drink industry the competitive position of the franchise bottler is often improved while that of the franchising firm is diminished.

One consequence has been a growing awareness among bottlers that their competitive interests often differ from those of the corporations that sell them syrup or concentrate and support the national brand name. Awareness has influenced decisions regarding advertising policy, product mix, packaging, and pricing in ways that go far beyond the effects of container regulation alone.

Cost Variability

Regulation can also have a significant impact on the variability of costs. The most obvious instances involve insurance-related issues. For example, workers' compensation laws helped reduce the variance in workers' claims against employers. By providing for a certain payment of a fixed amount, both employer and employee no longer have to cope with a process where payments are both uncertain and variable.

A more recent case involves airbags in automobiles. In the

absence of passive restraint regulation, insurers are now confronted with the prospect of relatively high claims for bodily injuries in the relatively few cases where serious accidents occur. For the majority of accidents, the absence of a triggered airbag, which needs to be repaired, means lower costs for property damage. This must be contrasted with a regulatory system that requires passive restraints. In that case, the relatively small number of large claims decreases, but the number of small property damage claims rises since passive restraints must be repaired. The payment of a comparably small and predictable property damage payment in a large number of accidents once airbags are installed is not unlike the relatively certain payment of a worker's compensation claim. There is considerable public debate as to whether the total social costs are higher or lower with or without a passive restraint policy. What is fairly clear, however, is that whatever happens to the level of these costs, the variability will likely drop with the installation of the restraints.

There are numerous opportunities for the public sector to intervene in private-sector affairs to achieve reductions in the variability of costs to the benefit of both producers and consumers. For example, the uncertainties associated with liability suits surrounding chemical substances (asbestos, agent orange, et cetera) subsequently proven harmful to health are substantial. There may well be opportunities for regulators to trade a predictable expense for a highly unpredictable court settlement in these instances.

Profits in the Value-Added Chain

The airbag and bottle bill examples also illustrate how changes in an industry's cost structure as a result of government regulations can shift the locus of profits in complex chains of product manufacture and distribution.

Consider first the soft-drink example. National franchise companies like Coca-Cola and PepsiCo manufacture a soft-drink syrup or concentrate that they then sell to independent or company-owned franchised bottlers. The bottlers, in turn, use the syrup to make soft drinks and then package and deliver them to consumers via a retail network.

The national company earns a profit on its syrup or concentrate sales. Of course, the more Coke is consumed the more profit to Coca-Cola. More important, however, because the profit margins on this syrup are typically fixed by contract, the national company requires more total sales volume to earn more profit. In the extreme, from the syrup producer's standpoint, it is worth sacrificing bottling profits—which producers do not get anyway—to sell more syrup—the profits of which producers do get.

In contrast, bottlers earn a higher profit on both higher sales volume *and* higher margin if they can price their product higher or reduce their costs. Bottlers, therefore, might actually be willing to sacrifice some case sales if it meant higher prices or lower costs and, consequently, higher total profits. The national company would not likely find lower case sales profitable, since profits are typically a fixed percentage of total sales volume.

In this competitive environment, the incentives of the national companies are clear: sell more volume, even if this means somewhat lower profits for bottlers. One manifestation of this tendency has been the proliferation of high-cost, but very attractive to the consumer, one-way containers—cans, plastic, and disposable glass. The consumer likes the convenience, buys more product, and the profits of syrup producers rise.

Bottlers' profits do not necessarily fare so well, however, since convenience containers are expensive to purchase. Unlike refillable containers that require a large, well-developed recycling system for cost-effectiveness, one-ways pose few entry barriers to new competitors. The result, of course, is aggressive price competition—which helps sell still more syrup but does not necessarily mean more bottler profits. Ostensibly, bottlers are protected by their exclusive franchise territory, but aggressive marketing by the national companies can help overcome this protective barrier.

Enter the "bottle bill." Now, by law, in some eleven different states even one-ways have a deposit to encourage their return. The process of collecting and possibly recycling containers is a labor-intensive activity so the competitive advantage accrues to those firms with the ability to efficiently and profitably manage labor and other distribution services at a local market level. This is, of course, a traditional strength of local bottlers. Regulation has thus created something of a competitive edge for the local bottler who controls this critical link in the chain of distribution. With this new competitive edge, bottlers may well decide to sacrifice some volume to attain higher total profits for themselves. This might occur by limiting the servicing of low-volume outlets or raising the prices on certain product lines. The point is that even the small shift in the competitive balance between bottler and franchiser can have profound impacts on the distribution of profits in the soft-drink industry. Such is often the case when government action upsets a delicate competitive equilibrium that has taken years to establish.

Whether total costs rise or fall in this industry with container regulation will likely be argued for years. The cost structure impact, however, is less ambiguous: the greater labor-intensity and increased importance of bottler-controlled avenues of distribution helps redirect the competitive balance from the national franchiser toward the franchisee. Profit potential, in other words, has been shifted among competitors in the value-added chain.

The airbag example is similar. Advocates and opponents of airbags will argue interminably over the impact of this technology on the total cost of auto services. But look at the issue strictly from a cost *structure* standpoint. According to William Nordhaus, a Yale economist testifying before Congress on behalf of several auto insurance companies, airbags increase the consumer cost of a new car by about $60. (General Motors says $80 or more.) Nordhaus also estimates, however, that insurance costs will drop by $30 annually. This is not a bad return on a

$60 to $80 investment. Airbags, in other words, may well lower the total cost of driving, as their advocates claim.[6]

Why, then, does General Motors oppose them? After all, lower total costs for driving will presumably mean higher total expenditures on automotive services, since lower prices always mean at least some stimulus to demand. In fact, if consumers behave in the future as they have in the past, they will respond to these lower costs not by pocketing the money but by increasing their expenditures on driving by a nearly equivalent amount —by buying fancier cars, driving more, and carrying better insurance.

What matters to General Motors, however, is how much of any change in consumer expenditures on automotive services it will get and to what extent it will offset the higher costs the firm will incur to install airbags. Because passive restraints do increase the cost of the *vehicle* relative to other automotive services, their mandatory purchase will encourage less frequent purchases of new cars and/or otherwise less costly vehicles. Thus, while any lowering of the total costs of driving will encourage greater consumption of automotive services, the relative increase in the price of the vehicle itself might reduce the automakers' *share* of these expenditures. Automakers' strong opposition to passive restraints clearly indicates that they believe the negative cost *structure* impact of this regulation dominates any beneficial consequences of lower total costs for automotive services that such restraints might imply. This conclusion is only reinforced, of course, by manufacturers' studies showing more cost-effective alternatives to achieve the same level of safety benefits.[7]

Once again, the critical competitive impact is not measured strictly by the level of costs due to government action. Rather it is measured by the change in the *structure* of costs and the corresponding consequences for the profitability of individual links in the chain of production and distribution of automotive services.

Conclusion

Managers in the private sector have long recognized that government intervention has a profound influence on competitive relationships. Too often these effects have been described strictly in terms of regulation's impacts on the cost of doing business. By focusing on costs, business managers have often failed to communicate the validity of their intuition. In this chapter we have seen many of the reasons why this intuition is, in many instances, correct. Public intervention in competitive markets has impacts that go well beyond those related to the higher cost of doing business. They have to do with changes in the capital intensity of doing business, the attendant risk of investment, and the consequences for international competitiveness. Public actions, their broader social merits or demerits notwithstanding, can upset delicate competitive equilibria in complex channels of distribution with major effects on both consumers and producers. All of these effects can occur even when public actions cause the cost of production to fall. In other words, to understand competition when government matters, it is essential to pay attention to far more than the direct cost of regulatory compliance.

Chapter 5

Capacity and Its Utilization

The last two chapters discussed the various ways government policy influences the level and structure of production costs: production capacity was taken as given. This chapter examines the role that government policy plays in decisions to expand, operate, and close production facilities.

There are at least three reasons for focusing on the capacity impacts of public actions. First, capacity decisions typically represent major capital commitments by private investors and, consequently, are important to the health of the economy at large as well as to the individual investor. And since capital assets are also long-lived, the economy must deal for many years with the inherited legacy of prior capacity decisions. Major industrial plant investments, for example, can have useful lives of 30 to 50 years, and many public infrastructure investments, such as dams or waterways, can have planned lives of 100 to 150 years. By virtue of their long-term strategic significance, capacity decisions are justifiably the object of considerable managerial and policy attention.

Second, capacity decisions are made relatively infrequently. While even the most vocal advocates of government intervention may be reluctant to undertake the administrative challenge of having the public sector participate in daily business decisions regarding production levels, operations management, or pricing, there may be no such reluctance to intervene in capacity decisions because they are relatively infrequent. Capacity decisions are, in other words, feasible candidates for regulatory intervention.

And third, the principal input to capacity decisions is capital, the one input factor most subject to manipulation and control —directly or otherwise—by public policy makers. This manipulation occurs through tax policy, savings policy, banking regulation, and the like.

In sum, capacity decisions would appear to be opportune targets for public policy makers' attention. Their importance is unquestioned, and their relative infrequency and dependence on capital inputs presumably would make it more feasible to place these decisions, rather than many other business decisions, under administrative control.

To see how public actions influence capacity decisions in industry, it is useful to examine two separate issues: the impact of government policy on existing capacity and the impact on new capacity. In the shorthand of regulatory impact analysis, the first problem is one of "retrofit" and the second is one of "new source performance."

The Retrofit Problem

The regulatory retrofit problem itself has two basic components. First, because existing facilities were not designed with some particular regulatory objective in mind—say, clean water or low noise levels—it is almost invariably more costly to achieve public policy objectives in existing facilities than in new ones that can be designed to deal with these social objectives. Robert Crandall of Brookings has estimated, for example, that pollution control adds 6.4 percent to the cost of expanding existing facilities in the steel industry but only 3.3 percent for entirely new plants.[1] And second, because of the cost of retrofitting, some facilities are likely to become uneconomic and thus be forced to close in the face of regulatory intervention.

HIGH RETROFIT COSTS

Even in the absence of the kind of confirming evidence Crandall has provided, we can assume that all other things being equal, retrofit costs are unlikely to be any cheaper than the costs of regulatory compliance in new facilities. The reason for this is simply that decision makers have more technological options available to them when designing new facilities than when working with existing facilities. Unless there are institutional reasons why new investments are penalized vis-a-vis retrofit investments—due, say, to grandfather regulatory provisions of one form or another, as will be discussed below—we would typically expect retrofitting to be a relatively expensive undertaking.

We would also expect retrofitting to be expensive for another reason. Existing facilities may have shorter remaining economic lives than new facilities. Given a shorter period of time to recoup retrofit costs, unit costs rise, either because management employs a low-cost, capital-intensive technology and is forced to recover the investment more quickly than in a new facility, or because management opts for a different technology which has a life span consistent with that of the existing plant.

This second point is especially important in regulatory settings since, as we observed in chapter 4, policy makers frequently try to impose regulations that minimize the "total life-cycle cost" of regulation—a concept based on the useful economic life of the required compliance technology. The useful life of such investments in practice, however, is not technology-specific but plant-specific. What represents the cheapest compliance method for a plant with a twenty-year remaining life is likely to differ from that of one with a three-year remaining life.

The resulting bias against old facilities increases the costs of regulation in existing plants. Because facilities with the shortest remaining lives are likely to be marginal competitors in an industry to begin with, this process can add disproportionately high compliance costs to already high-cost producers.

The result is exactly what you would expect given the normal interplay of supply and demand. The imposition of costly regulations increases the cost of doing business. Industry output drops with the resulting price increases, and marginal facilities are forced to close.

This characterization of the retrofit/plant closing problem is accurate as far as it goes, but it does not go far enough in three important dimensions. First, it ignores political responses to the high-cost retrofit problem; second, it ignores the economic impact on facilities that do not close; and third, it does not consider the dynamics of industrial adaptation over time.

POLITICS AND HIGH RETROFIT COSTS

In practice, public officials are often sensitive to the plight of an industry's marginal producers. As noted earlier, policy makers often impose less stringent rules upon them, perhaps by "subcategorizing" an industry along technological lines. Since facilities of a similar vintage frequently employ a similar technology, this is a convenient device to single out high-cost compliers and relax standards accordingly.

Given that these facilities, by virtue of being an industry's marginal suppliers, also determine the resulting price consequences of regulation, there is added political incentive to reduce these costs substantially. By so doing, a regulator can lower the price impact of regulation to consumers and reduce the likelihood of plant closings at the same time. Such a policy, it must be stressed, necessarily works to the competitive disadvantage of otherwise low-cost sources of compliance that are forced to bear the full cost burden of regulation but get less offsetting price relief. Thus the regulator's sensitivity to the plight of marginal producers and the political paranoia that typically surrounds the plant closing problem has the peculiar indirect effect of decreasing the comparative advantage regulation would otherwise be expected to bestow on low-cost competitors.

The policy maker's dilemma, of course, is that a policy which affords general price relief for the industry disadvantages consumers (via higher prices) and exacerbates the plant-closing problem by reducing demand. Given these trade-offs, it would not be surprising to see regulators opting for policies that create lower price increases and fewer plant closings.

CAPACITY CURTAILMENTS WITHOUT PLANT CLOSINGS

Plant closings, however, are not the only source of capacity curtailments due to regulation. Facilities that do not close can move to lower capacity levels after regulation is imposed. To illustrate, a lead refinery I once visited had a serious air pollution problem and needed to install a stack scrubber to reduce the level of its emissions. Because the lead industry was experiencing excess capacity, there was no desire to scale the scrubber to the facility's existing output potential. There was, on the other hand, no desire to close the facility. The solution was to install a relatively small-scale scrubber that would allow the plant's ore sintering operation to run at only 75 percent of its rated capacity. Since ore sintering is basic to lead making, a 25 percent capacity reduction in this process was equivalent to an overall reduction in capacity of 25 percent.

This facility, in other words, did not close but its capacity fell substantially. There is no reason to believe that this is an isolated example. To the contrary, it is reasonable to expect that any management confronting the decision to commit capital investment to an existing facility will carefully reconsider the merits of a continuing commitment to the scale of the facility.

There are two important economic implications of these efforts to rationalize capacity in the face of regulatory intervention. First, they reduce available industry capacity even though discrete facilities may not close. Like all capacity reductions, this can put upward pressure on an industry's prices. Second, these decisions can impart an important degree of short-run inelasticity to supply. That is, with reductions in available capacity, the industry will be less able to respond quickly to cyclical increases in demand. The resulting loss in supply flexibility can add substantially to an industry's overall price volatility.

Consider the example of lead once again. The consumption of lead has declined from 1.36 million tons in 1970 to 1.19 million tons in 1982.[2] This reduction is itself a consequence of regulations restricting the use of lead in gasoline, paints, and so forth. In the absence of offsetting capacity reductions, reduced demand would imply excess productive capacity. With high fixed costs and low capacity utilization, competitors would be strongly tempted to reduce prices to expand volume, especially in weak markets. Even with the kinds of regulatory-induced capacity reductions just described, the average price of lead in New York, adjusted for inflation, fell from 15.96 cents per pound in 1970 to 11.11 cents per pound in 1982.[3]

DYNAMICS OF CAPACITY CURTAILMENTS

In high fixed cost settings like the lead industry, the conventional expectation is that losses incurred in recessions will be offset by high profits in cyclical peaks of economic activity. With the overhang of capacity, however, the good times are less likely to come, because as demand increases, there is considerable supply available to meet it. This "elastic" short-run supply prevents firms from recovering the losses experienced in cyclical troughs. Such a circumstance has characterized the domestic steel industry for some time. Low profits in downturns have not been offset by high profits during peaks due to excess steelmaking capacity worldwide.

If, however, government actions force managers to seriously reconsider their commitments to existing capacity and encourage them to close or reduce the output potential of existing plants, supply is made less elastic in the short run and losses are more likely to be recovered when markets expand.

The petroleum refining industry illustrates this phenomenon. Historically—in the 1950s and 1960s—when oil was plentiful and cheap, integrated petroleum producers adopted capacity strategies that looked something like this: large multinational corporations expanded into crude oil production where the barriers to entry to new competition were highest and, thus, profits were sustainable at reasonably high levels. They then built substantial refining capacity, often in anticipation of demand growth, a strategy that had two effects. First, it discouraged the entry of other firms into this sector of the business—after all, industry segments with abundant capacity relative to demand rarely generate the kinds of profits that justify substantial risk capital commitments.

Second, as these refineries tried to operate profitably and recover their high fixed costs, they found it attractive to bid aggressively for crude oil at the same time they cut prices to consumers to increase volume. This expanded the profits at the wellhead at the same time it kept customers happy. This aggressive capacity expansion strategy was attractive only so long as energy was cheap, profits at the wellhead more than offset any losses at the refinery, and demand could be stimulated through price reduction.

In the 1970s this strategy became less attractive. The Organization of Petroleum Exporting Countries (OPEC) and other producing nations "discovered" their ability to capture the wellhead profits for themselves and indeed to increase prices substantially. The resulting higher prices to consumers lowered demand for refined products, adding to the surplus of refining capacity relative to demand.

Integrated oil producers, who owned both crude oil production and refining capacity, thus faced a dilemma. Competitive pressures to utilize refining capacity would merely shift profits back to the wellhead and thus to foreign governments. There was a clear need to reduce the glut in refining capability to restore profitability. Of course, an individual competitor could close a refinery—and dozens did—but to do so would always sacrifice a large capital investment primarily for the benefit of competitors who kept their facilities open.

Enter government. The Clean Air Act encouraged the Environmental Protection Agency to examine catalytic converter technology for automobile exhaust emissions controls. These converters required the use of unleaded gasoline. While U.S. oil refiners had excess capacity in the aggregate, they possessed relatively limited capacity to produce unleaded gasoline; moreover, the use of existing facilities to produce it would effectively reduce the productive capacity of prior refinery investments, because unleaded gasoline requires more intensive processing than leaded gasoline.

While this situation might have been expected to create an outpouring of opposition, in fact, such forced—and coordinated —obsolescence of substantial refining capacity may well have served the industry's competitive interests. This is not to say that regulation was a boon to this industry, but only that the capacity consequences of regulation helped offset at least some of the negative competitive consequences of regulatory intervention and other changes in the market environment.

As we saw earlier, President Reagan's first Administrator of the EPA, Anne Gorsuch, discovered this reality the hard way when she attempted to relax the standards for lead in gasoline. Such a relaxation would have increased the effective capacity of the refining industry and substantially increased the short-run elasticity of supply at the very time the capacity glut was already depressing profits. The Gorsuch deregulation scheme fit the strategy of the 1960s but not the strategic realities of the 1980s.

Once the capacity impacts of government actions are carefully considered in a competitive context, it is sometimes possible to find usually opposing industrial and social interest groups on the same side of a policy issue.

The Problem of Capital Diversion

In addition to affecting existing facilities, regulations have an impact on new investments. According to one point of view, public actions can stymie the expansion of supply by diverting capital that might otherwise be used for capacity expansion to regulatory compliance. According to this argument, the need to invest in plant and equipment to meet mandated government requirements reduces the amount of capital available for investment in so-called productive facilities. While there are many things wrong with this conventional argument, there are also a number of things right about it.

Advocates of the capital diversion argument often assume— implicitly or otherwise—that the total supply of investment funds is fixed. Because compliance investments are allegedly "required," they presumbly reduce the net investment available for so-called productive investment. Both of these implicit assumptions are misleading.

In fact, the funds available for investment are not fixed. They rise and fall with cash flow, interest rates, stock performance, and the like. Moreover, no compliance investment is "required"; there is always the option of retiring a facility—or in the extreme, bankruptcy—rather than bringing it up to regulatory standards. Failure to realize that investment levels are not fixed can—and does—produce major misreadings of the competitive effects of public policy.

Consider, first, the regulatory factors that might deplete sources of investment funds. If regulatory compliance exhibits economies of scale and leads to an increase in minimum efficient scale of new facilities, for example, this may increase the riskiness of investments in new facilities. Increased risk, all other things being equal, will increase the cost of capital and thereby reduce total investment—a reduction unrelated to the magnitude of any capital "diverted" to compliance investments.

It is often the case that industry views regulatory investments as "required," not because they are literally mandated by law but because the alternative—closing existing facilities—is unacceptable. From the standpoint of incremental investment decisions, these compliance investments are often quite "profitable" in the sense that they allow industry to continue to earn returns on earlier investments. On a total profitability basis, however, these "profits" do not exist, of course. They exist only in the sense that the losses would be greater if compliance did not occur. Any resulting loss in total profitability, however, comes at the expense of equity owners. This loss to them can discourage equity investments and thus further reduce the sum of money available for investment—again, independent of any impact due to capital diversion itself.

But just as there are factors that decrease investment funds, there are factors that increase them. For example, if regulation causes some existing firms to close or increases the incremental costs of production most for an industry's marginal producers, some competitors—the winners—will experience revenue increases that exceed cost increases due to regulation. This added cash flow will increase the funds available for investment.

The net impacts of regulation on investment are difficult to disentangle and by no means limited to the simple logic of capital diversion. Researchers at the National Bureau of Economic Research (NBER) illustrated this in a study of the impact of water pollution control on investment in the paper industry. In their study, analysts simulated the investment consequences of two extreme cases.[4]

In the first case, total available investment was assumed to be constrained entirely by the industry's cash flow. Thus pollution control investments decreased the money available for new capacity dollar for dollar for a given level of cash flow. The NBER analysts, however, did allow the level of cash flow to fluctuate with the price changes and capacity shutdowns precipitated by regulation. The simulated pattern of net investment revealed that capital diversion was in some ways self-correcting, for as new facilities were *not* built due to diversion of capital, prices would rise, generating some offsetting cash flow.

In the second scenario, the industry was presumed to invest so long as money could be acquired from capital markets, through either debt or equity, at a cost less than the return on new facilities and through added cash flow. This investment pool was substantially larger than the first pool.

With investment levels differing substantially in the two scenarios, industry capacity levels and corresponding price and output levels differed substantially as well. According to these simulations, if full capital diversion occurred, as many in industry feared, the reduction in effective industry capacity would yield substantial short-run price increases. In contrast, if added investment was forthcoming, the industry's capital stock would adapt to the new circumstances much more quickly, with substantially lower price increases. The reason for this latter impact, of course, is that new facilities would employ the latest cost-saving technology.

Note that from a public perspective, the more rapidly the capital stock is turned over, the lower the long-run price effects of regulatory policy but the greater the near-term pain for consumers. The long-term price effects are favorable because new facilities use the latest technology, and the more rapid the rollover of the capital stock, the more new technology is in place; the near-term pain is the greatest because of the high price increases to consumers necessary to finance this new investment. This poses a real—and a not infrequent—choice for policy makers.

An analogous situation occurred with rising energy prices. Policy makers had to choose between a gradual versus a sudden increase. The gradual increase reduced the current pain, and from a political standpoint it is not surprising that this path was chosen. But a gradual adjustment to higher prices also deferred the day in which the economy would have fully adapted to the long-run realities of higher energy prices. We are, for example, still driving fuel-inefficient automobiles purchased in the mid-1970s when gasoline prices were kept artificially low. We would have a more fuel-efficient auto fleet today if we had endured greater pain in the 1970s. But who is to say that the pain would have justified the benefits?

New Source Performance Standards

The impact of government policy on capacity is perhaps clearest in the case of stringent new source performance standards that require new facilities to meet regulatory standards much tougher than those of new facilities. The rationale for such practices is clear: it is presumed to be inequitable to require investors who made "good-faith" investments in the past to bear a costly regulatory burden; the political pressure to keep financial pressure off existing facilities is always strong; and new facilities are implicitly assumed to be able to "afford" costly regulatory compliance costs.

It is this last point that needs our attention, for its validity rests on the implicit assumption that new capacity has a competitive advantage over old capacity. According to this logic, new facilities earn substantial profits, or what economists call "quasi-rents." High regulatory compliance costs merely tax these rents, but do not otherwise discourage new investments.

The logic of this argument is persuasive only so long as new capacity is at a competitive advantage. This may not be the case, however, for a variety of reasons. For example, new facilities face high capital costs relative to historic averages, must choose from a diminishing supply of attractive sites, and often require such large scale to be cost-competitive that they represent high-risk investments. In this situation, existing capacity with low embedded capital costs, advantageous locations, and often a regulatory preference are at an advantage.

The competitive consequences of new capacity being placed at a cost disadvantage by public policy can be substantial and go well beyond minor changes in the profitability of individual investments. They can, in fact, fundamentally alter the face of competition in an industry.

Capacity Strategies—A Private-Sector Perspective

To see how substantial the competitive effects of new source biases can be in theory, it is first necessary to consider how the role of new capacity differs in various industries.

THE LOW-COST CASE

When regulation makes new capacity low cost relative to existing facilities, it becomes desirable to build new large-scale facilities to exploit this cost advantage. It is frequently advisable to build these facilities ahead of the growth in demand to preempt competitive entry and to force those price reductions that will make demand expansion self-fulfilling.

In these circumstances, it makes sense to debt-finance new investments because their low costs will assure a high rate of capacity utilization and there is little danger of excessive operating leverage. Because costs are low, it is attractive to compete on the basis of price. It is unattractive to expand by acquisition, since existing facilities are high cost; the retrofitting of existing facilities similarly makes less economic sense.[5]

THE HIGH-COST CASE

When regulation makes new facilities high cost relative to existing ones, the strategic implications change by 180 degrees. It is not attractive to build big facilities; it is better to build small to avoid the underutilization of expensive equipment. Rather than build in anticipation of market growth, it is better to wait for growth to occur. When new facilities are high cost, it is best not to risk operating leverage; rather, technologies with low fixed costs are preferred, even if it means relatively high variable costs of production. In these circumstances, expansion by acquiring existing facilities is preferred to building high-cost new ones, as is competition on bases other than price.

The implications of these two cases are dramatically different for policy makers as well as for competitive strategists. For example, when new facilities are low cost and industry is pursuing aggressive capacity expansion strategies, there is little risk of stimulative macroeconomic policies triggering inflation since ample, low-cost capacity is readily available. If new facilities are cheap enough, then stringent regulatory requirements on new facilities will be a painless way to bring society into compliance with various regulatory demands, since the cost of such constraints will merely reduce the otherwise high profits of new investments.

The consequences of regulatory biases against new sources of supply are not merely theoretical. The empirical evidence shows that the effects are real, significant, and often unintended, as two cases will show.

THE AUTO CASE

Emissions control requirements are mandated for new cars but not required for automobiles manufactured prior to the date of regulation. While most of us consider this a sensible rule—after all, the cost of retrofitting the entire stock of existing cars would be colossal—this practice makes new cars more expensive than old ones, thus discouraging investments in new cars.

Professor Howard Gruenspecht of Carnegie-Mellon University has estimated the magnitude of this impact.[6] According to his estimates, a new car meeting 1981 auto emissions standards, compared to less stringent 1980 standards cost an additional $475. Gruenspecht estimated that this reduced new auto sales in the U.S. by almost 4 percent in 1981. Because fewer of the very clean new cars were sold, he also estimated that in 1984 the air actually contained more hydrocarbons and more carbon monoxide (but fewer nitrogen oxides) than it would have if the less stringent 1980 standard had applied. Over the long run, of course, the more stringent 1981 standard results in cleaner air, but not until the full effects of the new source bias are overcome sometime in 1985.

THE NEWSPRINT CASE

The second case involves the newsprint industry. Newsprint manufacturing is a highly polluting activity. When the Clean Water Act was passed in 1972, this industry was hit with expensive regulations. The burden on new capacity was sufficiently high that Arthur D. Little, Inc., estimated that in 1974 investments in new newsprint manufacturing facilities which met the tough new standards would earn only about 4 percent per year *before* tax. Despite newsprint shortages and escalating prices, it is not surprising that few newsprint facilities were built in the mid-1970s.[7]

As time passed, however, two events helped change this picture. First, regulations began to take hold on existing facilities. By itself, this helped to reduce the bias against new sources of supply. Second, energy prices skyrocketed. Energy is a major input to this industry. Ironically, while rising energy prices increased the total cost of newsprint manufacturing, they actually improved the *relative* cost of manufacturing newsprint in new facilities, which tend to use the latest and most energy-efficient technologies. Thus, rising energy costs helped overcome the new source bias created by environmental regulations, and by the late 1970s and early 1980s there was actually something of a boom in newsprint investment in North America.[8]

The impact of government policy on productive capacity can be substantial, with numerous strategic implications for the profitability, timing, and scale of new investments. By shaping the relative competitive position of new versus existing capacity, policy interventions can materially influence the pattern of capital expansion and the terms of competition in addition to their more generally recognized impacts on total costs and prices. The implications of these capacity impacts are not restricted to managers in the private sector but are important to public policy makers as well.

Capacity Strategies—A Public-Sector Perspective

Regulatory policies that affect the capacity strategies of private-sector firms also have implications for the capacity strategies of the public sector. Perhaps the easiest way to illustrate the strategic significance of these issues for the public sector is by the example of policies regarding import restrictions. While import restrictions do not reduce actual physical supply in the same way as an unleaded gasoline requirement, they do restrict effective supply in the protected market. Indeed, that is the source of their attraction to advocates of protection and the source of the objection by those opposed.

What is often ignored in these discussions is the fact that such policies not only restrict aggregate supply but, depending on how these restrictions are imposed, they also influence the short-run elasticity of supply and consequently have major competitive implications. Consider the different competitive effects of tariffs and quotas—two policies frequently advocated to protect domestic industries.

In a world where there are no import restraints, the supply of goods in the domestic market is merely the sum of the domestic and the foreign sources of supply. Such an unrestrained market not only yields the lowest possible prices to consumers but creates the largest possible pool of capacity available to serve cyclical peaks in demand. This relatively elastic supply tends to keep prices to consumers in check even in buoyant markets.

Now consider the imposition of a protective tariff, which effectively reduces the willingness of foreign suppliers to bring goods into the United States for any given price. This reduces total supply available to domestic consumers but does not otherwise impart any particular inelasticity to increases in supply when favorable shifts in demand occur. Indeed, once the price is high enough for foreign producers to justify the tariff, they are likely able to justify further supply as prices increase. One of the reasons domestic producers seeking trade restraint often oppose tariffs is related to this fact: as demand increases, the benefits of trade restraint based on tariffs are less than the benefits of using alternative regulatory mechanisms.

An example involves restrictions on imports by the imposition of a quota. Under such a scheme, no matter what the price, above a certain volume level, no imports are allowed. Now, a quota level can be chosen so that the resulting short-run price increase to consumers would be identical to that induced by a tariff. Ostensibly both policies would yield the same result— but only if demand conditions remain unchanged.

If demand changes, the results differ substantially under the two policies. Suppose demand increases. Under the tariff policy, the foreign producers are permitted to expand supply, provided they pay the tariff. They are prohibited from doing so under a quota system. The short-run elasticity of supply is much less under the quota than under the tariff policy; so the resulting price increases attributable to trade restraint are substantially greater with the quota than with the tariff policy.

Consider the competitive implications. Under the quota system, domestic price and volume levels are much more sensitive to demand fluctuations, encouraging competitive strategies that insulate domestic firms from price swings and cyclical swings in capacity utilization. In contrast, such swings are dampened substantially under a tariff system, which creates less downside risk to domestic firms at the same time it reduces upside potential.

Domestic competitors are far from indifferent to these two policies, even though they might both be designed to yield identical price and output impacts in the short run. Whether one policy will be preferred over the other depends on the competitive circumstances facing an individual competitor. If fixed costs are low, for example, and the costs of downswings in demand negligible, a competitor might prefer the quota policy, which offers considerable upside potential. If fixed costs are high and declines in demand a serious threat, the same competitor might prefer the tariff policy with its less volatile price and demand attributes.

Domestic competitors are also not indifferent to these two policies for political reasons. There are usually two sources of political opposition to trade restraint: consumers and foreign producers. A policy designed to make consumers pay higher prices is unlikely to ever earn their enthusiasm, so given the choice between two policies with similar adverse effects on consumers, the political stance of foreign suppliers becomes important. With tariffs, consumer prices rise, but much of the higher revenue accrues to the government in the form of tariff income. In the case of a quota having an identical impact on consumers, the revenue flows to foreign suppliers as well as to domestic firms. Thus, while foreign suppliers would generally prefer no trade restraint, they are typically less hostile to quotas than tariffs. Domestic producers often address the politics of this situation by supporting quotas.

Policy makers are not indifferent to these policy choices either. President Carter, for example, was considering the imposition of steel import restraints during his reelection campaign, and at the same time he was trying to fight inflation. Knowing that political pressures during election years encourage economic policy makers to err on the side of stimulation, it made sense to proffer import relief to the steel industry in the form of so-called trigger prices. The trigger or reference price system Carter proposed set a minimum price level below which steel could not be imported to the United States. Such a policy yielded a substantially greater degree of short-run elasticity of supply than either quotas or tariffs because once the floor level was exceeded, there were no restraints on foreign supply. Industry, not surprisingly, preferred the quota system, which offered the opportunity to take advantage of likely "errors" in economic stimulus.[9]

Conclusion

While much of the public discussion of government's impact on business involves the cost of regulation, many of the important competitive consequences of public policy are tied to its impact on both existing and new productive facilities. In this chapter we have seen the nature of these effects. The challenge to owners of existing facilities that confront high retrofit costs is very different from the challenge to new investors attempting to deal with the barriers posed by new source performance requirements. From the standpoint of the public policy maker, the resolution of these competing competitive interests is complicated by the overarching need to protect the broader interests of the nation's economy. Clearly, these are difficult policy challenges that merit thoughtful study more than inflammatory rhetoric.

Chapter 6

Public Policy
and Corporate Strategy

Earlier we discussed the competitive consequences of public policies stemming from intraindustry cost differentials and capacity impacts. In markets where competition stresses product differentiation, the competitive effects of public policy need not always show up in the form of significant capacity impacts or intraindustry cost differentials. In these industries corporate strategy—market niche strategy, in particular—can be an important determinant of the competitive consequences of public actions. Here we look in some detail at the interdependence of corporate strategy and public policy. While the focus is on strategy rather than cost, the mechanism creating the competitive impacts is the same in both cases: the Iron Law of Public Policy. Whether it is the cost of doing business or the strategy for competing in the marketplace, the competitive impacts of public policy stem from their differential effects on individual competitors.

The Concept of Strategy

To begin our discussion, it is useful to ask what a "strategy" is and why corporations have them. A corporate strategy is nothing more than management's plan for marshaling its limited resources to achieve the firm's objectives—financial and otherwise—over some planning horizon.[1] The need for a strategy is based on two elementary propositions, both of which are critical to the understanding of government's impact on business. The first is that no organization can be expected do all things well. Consequently, management typically must choose what skills the firm will try to cultivate and exploit competitively—and indirectly, the weaknesses the firm will also possess. Thus management must ultimately decide which market opportunities it will try to exploit and which it will leave to others. In today's economy there are profit-making opportunities in both hamburgers and personal computers, but few firms would be advised to attack both markets.

The second elemental proposition of corporate strategy is that competitive success depends on the ability of one firm to differentiate its product from that of its competition in the marketplace. Thus Burger King broils a hamburger to distinguish it from a fried McDonald's hamburger. Because competitive success stems from the ability to differentiate products on the marketing side of the business, and organizational success depends on the explicit choice of a limited number of organizational strengths, it follows that good strategy entails the proper matching of a firm's necessarily limited organizational skills with its marketing orientation.

In attempting to understand competition when government matters, the key consequence of strategic decision making is that individual firms, employing carefully matched marketing and organizational strategies that are intentionally differentiated from those of their competition, will necessarily face the competitive consequences of public regulatory actions from fundamentally different positions. Thus, just as earlier chapters showed that supposedly "uniform" public policies have differential competitive effects because of differential cost impacts, they also have differential competitive effects because of competing firms' different strategic positions.

Moreover, public policies place their own demands on the political, marketing, and technical skills of the corporation. Those firms that, by strategic design, possess the particular skills demanded by public action are affected differently from those that have elected to exploit other organizational capacities.

The implication is clear. The development of a corporate strategy is not only an overwhelming factor in shaping the firm's ability to create and respond to change in the marketplace, as it determines how the firm will participate competitively in an industry, what resources it will develop and deploy, and how it will coordinate and control these resources. It is also a critical factor in determining the firm's ability to respond to competitive challenges in a world in which government matters. Indeed, it may be the choice of strategy more than anything else that affects the firm's assessment of regulatory risk and its ability and inclination to cope effectively with public policy.

Scope of Participation in the Marketplace

A competitor's strategic choices concerning its scope of participation in any business are perhaps the most identifiable attributes of its strategy. These include choices regarding breadth of product line on the marketing side of the business. For example, some firms offer a full range of products across all market segments, while others compete in only some particular segment where they have a unique advantage.

Strategic product line decisions have important implications for the competitive effects of public actions. In the case of automobile manufacturers, General Motors (GM) confronts the regulatory requirement to satisfy congressionally mandated corporate average fuel economy (CAFE) standards very differently from Chrysler or Saab. GM has a broad product line but one that is tilted toward larger and lower-gas-mileage vehicles. Chrysler has a broad product line that includes a large share of fuel-efficient models. And Saab, by contrast, has a limited product line of mostly larger luxury vehicles. Thus the Saab Turbo can have higher fuel economy than the Chevrolet Corvette, but it is still possible for Saab to be in violation of fuel-economy standards. Why? Because GM also sells high-mileage Chevettes, which improve its overall corporate average fuel economy.[2]

A competitor's strategic choices also involve vertical integration decisions, which can also be shaped directly by public policies. Vertical integration in this context refers to the extent a firm is involved in the production and ownership of various intermediate production goods and raw materials. Thus some auto makers purchase parts while others make their own; some paper companies purchase wood pulp while others grow their own trees. In addition, a firm's vertical integration strategy has implications for its exposure to other aspects of regulatory change. Ford Motor Company, as a case in point, manufactures steel as well as automobiles. As a consequence, Ford is exposed to public policies directed at the steel industry that are very different from those GM experiences.[3]

In the early 1970s, for example, environmental control policies imposed substantial capital costs on steel manufacturers. Even if these costs were subsequently recovered in the form of higher prices, there was likely to be a differential competitive impact on Ford and GM. Ford, as a steelmaker, had to raise capital to comply with regulations, while GM saw the same environmentally related cost increase as a higher operating cost. As a consequence of the two different strategies, Ford confronted higher fixed costs of doing business and a greater exposure to the financial risks of a cyclical downturn in the auto market that resulted from a higher fixed-cost structure. In contrast, GM saw its variable costs rise but its fixed costs and operating leverage little changed.

The regulatory exposure was not all favorable to GM, however. Government-imposed import restraints affected the steel industry at the same time that it faced environmental regulations. To the extent these restraints drove up the price of steel, Ford was protected—indeed, may have actually benefited—while GM saw its raw material prices rise.

The point is not that one vertical integration strategy was necessarily preferable to the other but rather that each strategy exposed the firm pursuing it to different competitive consequences when public regulatory actions were taken.

Other Dimensions of Strategic Impact

The successful marketing of most consumer products requires a sales, service, and distribution network and, in the case of consumer durables like automobiles and appliances, often a financing ability. All these activities are in addition to a firm's manufacturing capability. The fact that often significant regulatory constraints dictate the ways in which these activities can be organized is particularly critical to a consideration of government's impact on business. For example, for many years railroads were prohibited from providing a broad range of transportation services by regulations that forbade the simultaneous ownership of rail and trucking capabilities. Similarly, restrictions on the advertising of medical and legal services have shaped both of these industries in important ways, as have regulatory limitations on the activities of financial institutions and telecommunications service providers.

One interesting example of the ways in which government policy can influence firms with different strategies involves the Kodak and Polaroid corporations. Antitrust policies place restrictions on the tied sale of film and its processing. Technically, these regulations apply to all competitors, but as always happens with the Iron Law, some firms win and others lose. Thus Kodak may be prevented from tying processing to the sale of its film, but Polaroid, due to the technical innovation of self-developing film, was not subject to this regulatory constraint. You cannot buy Polaroid film without simultaneously purchasing the film's processing.

Not all competitors choose to compete on the same basis. Thus some firms will emphasize product performance, others, price competition. Both of these strategies are affected by government action but in dramatically different ways. The price-competitive manufacturer is much more affected by the impact of regulation on the cost of doing business, while the performance-oriented producer is less affected by the cost increases associated with regulation but may be seriously affected by the delays in new product innovation created by licensing and permit requirements. The key point is that the election of different competitive emphases by different firms leads to a different exposure to the competitive consequences of public policy decisions.

Still another set of strategic business choices relates to the management of change. The contrast between European and American automobile producers in the 1950s and 1960s illustrates the nature of the alternatives managers confront. Competitive development in the U.S. automobile market had historically led to the choice of body styling and sheet-metal forming as the way of introducing change. In this environment, engines, transmission, and other power-train components remained highly standardized and modularized to accommodate change in associated body configurations without disrupting economies of scale. Historically, however, the European industry developed with a different competitive emphasis: body fabrication tended much more toward standardization, while change centered on performance, particularly with reference to handling and speed.

These differing approaches to change were especially important when environmental regulations were promulgated, for these rules necessitated dramatic technological changes that were far from incremental in nature. Thus U.S. producers not only confronted the technological, economic, and marketing challenges of regulatory compliance, but did so with organizations that had different capacities for change than those required by public policy.

This last point is critically important because it illustrates that the transitional problems of coping with public policy are not necessarily indicative of poor management; rather, they can simply reflect the legacy of organizational skills with which management must confront new policy initiatives.[4]

Federal Energy Policy and Competitive Strategy in the U.S. Automobile Industry

To illustrate the ways in which public policy exposes firms with different corporate strategies to different competitive consequences, consider the impact of federal energy and trade policies on the automobile industry in the United States.[5]

U.S. automobile manufacturers have faced unprecedented pressures for change in the last fifteen years. Some of these pressures are the direct result of government actions in the environmental and safety areas. At the same time these regulatory policies have been put in place, international competition and a highly cyclical domestic economy have posed challenges to this capital-intensive industry. While the industry was experiencing these environmental changes, competitors also confronted dramatic change in federal energy policies. As will be discussed, these policies had a profound impact on each domestic producer; the nature of this impact was determined largely by the corporate strategies in place at the time these public policy actions were initiated.

In December 1975 the Energy Policy and Conservation Act

(EPCA) became Public Law 94-163. This act established mandatory efficiency standards regulating the average mileage of each automobile company's fleet produced or sold in the United States during any given model year. These corporate average fuel economy, or CAFE, standards included 18 miles per gallon (mpg) for the model year 1978, 19 mpg for 1979, 20 mpg for 1980, and 27.5 mpg for 1985 and years following. The act authorized the National Highway Traffic Safety Administration (NHTSA) to set standards for the model years between 1980 and 1995; 22 mpg was prescribed for 1984. The estimated average fuel economy for the entire 1977 fleet of domestically produced models was 17.7 mpg; new models achieved an average of 18.6 mpg. Failure to meet the prescribed fleet-weighted averages was to result in a fine of $5 assessed to the manufacturer for every tenth of a mile each car in the fleet fell below the mandated standards.

In subsequent legislation Congress twice modified the regulatory structure of the law. The National Energy and Conservation Act of 1978—Public Law 95-619—increased the sanctions for noncompliance and raised the potential penalty to $10 for every tenth of a mile. Then, in an effort to ease the industry's difficulties, the Automotive Fuel Efficiency Act of 1980 permitted auto manufacturers to carry credits for surpassing the annual efficiency standard three years forward or three years backward to compensate for any shortfalls. And in 1985, by administrative action NHTSA changed the CAFE requirement for model year 1986 to 26.0 mpg. Even with these legislative and administrative changes, since 1975 the EPCA has remained the cornerstone of government's efforts to induce greater fuel efficiency in American automobiles.

To understand the strategic business implications of the CAFE standards, it is first necessary to understand the political pressures that led the government away from higher gasoline prices and toward a regulatory approach to fuel economy.

In the months following the oil shock of 1973–74, the debate in Congress over the decontrol of oil prices was extensive and complex. Opinion polls at the time showed that half the people surveyed believed there never was an energy crisis but rather that the oil companies were to blame for skyrocketing prices. In addition to problems of public skepticism, the public perceived oil price decontrol as a major threat to the nation's ailing economy. Faced with what Representative Al Ullman called an "invisible crisis" and the fear of the economic implications of higher gasoline prices, Congress turned to gasoline price control as the political solution to both problems. The relationship between this regulatory policy and the strategic orientation of the domestic automobile firms can be seen more clearly by examining the actual experience of individual automotive producers.

GENERAL MOTORS CORPORATION

Historically, the GM product strategy had emphasized "a car for every purse and purpose." GM had always led the inter- mediate- and standard-size U.S. markets, especially in the high- er-priced, higher-profit ranges, while also providing a maxi- mum range of choice. In some, though not all, segments of the U.S. market, GM had been the leader in pricing, styling, and innovation. The firm had been particularly successful in selling luxury options such as automatic transmissions, air condition- ers, and power steering.

As the U.S. market first began to change in the latter part of the 1960s, GM began to lose its market share. In response to increased purchases of small cars, GM introduced the Vega and reduced its emphasis on annual model changes. The company reduced the number of models from 140 to 134 and announced that the Chevette design would remain unchanged for a number of years. In 1974 GM's market share dropped several percentage points in one year despite large advertising expenditures. By the end of 1974 sales were down 34 percent. In the autumn of 1974 GM announced its down-sizing program. (Actually this was preceded by two other decisions in late 1973 to intro- duce the Chevette and the down-size Cadillac Seville.) The Chevette was designed to counter small-size imports while the

Seville was positioned against Mercedes-Benz. The Chevette had marked the apparent determination by GM to become the world's major producer of small cars.

Down-sizing was a crucial decision for General Motors. The firm's product strategy had always been to provide a wide variety of consumer choices while focusing on family-size cars and the luxury market. GM management chose to down-size from the top of the line—that is, to down-size larger cars first—to protect the diversity of the product mix. The company presumably felt it would be easier to redefine the market's idea of a family-size car and keep customers in them than to try to switch them immediately to a new small car. Down-sizing from the top maintained the continuity of the GM line and allowed customers to stay with the familiar GM name. It also avoided opening a gap in the line and confusing everyone if the down-sizing had been done at the low end only. The decision to undertake what GM executive Thomas A. Murphy called "the most comprehensive, ambitious, far-reaching, costly program of its kind in the history of our industry" reflected management's understanding of the energy problem and its willingness to commit the requisite capital. Between 1975 and 1979 GM spent almost $3.2 billion a year in the first half of two projected down-sizings scheduled before 1985. All full-size and intermediate GM cars were reproportioned before Ford and Chrysler produced their first down-size cars in 1979.

GM's strategic response to the EPCA can be viewed in the context of this overall down-sizing strategy. Down-sizing had two advantages. First, it would acclimate current customers to the new economic realities; and second, it would facilitate interim compliance with CAFE standards. Thus the GM strategy was conditioned substantially by its existing market orientation.

In manufacturing the intermediate-size X-body cars in the spring of 1979 in quantities substantially greater than prevailing or projected gasoline prices seemed to warrant, GM appeared to have opted for excess capacity. However, since market circumstances dramatically changed just as these vehicles were introduced, what was thought to be excess capacity was, in reality insufficient capacity.

Given GM's strategic interest in maintaining a diversified product line and broad customer base, the cost of down-sizing would likely have been incurred with or without the EPCA, but perhaps not as rapidly. Similarly, uncertainties in GM's market-place also argued for flexibility in manufacturing capacity, which the firm actually sought. Overall, the EPCA policy and GM's strategic orientation were relatively well synchronized.

GM's strategy, however, did leave it vulnerable to some com-petitive threats and indirect costs from the EPCA. For example, the GM strategy was a clear victim of the regulation-induced upgrading of the Japanese product lines. This upgrading was a result of CAFE mileage standards that, when combined with low regulated gasoline prices, meant that it was generally less profitable to sell small cars—because gasoline was so cheap—but more profitable to sell large ones. Consequently, the Japa-nese, whose competitive orientation was in the small-car mar-ket, had a strong incentive to upgrade their lines into larger cars to maintain profitability.

Now, this is not to say that the Japanese had no other incen-tives to upgrade their car lines. Rather, federal energy policy directly complemented the strategic Japanese interest in moving to upscale car sales in the U.S. market.

This argument suggests that GM's own strategy was not dramatically affected by federal energy policy, but that the firm was affected indirectly by the strategic incentives given to some of its major competitors. There is, of course, an alternative argument: that without the pace of down-sizing the EPCA forced on GM, the firm would be in a much worse strategic position today compared with Japanese competition. For this argument to be true, it is necessary to believe that GM would have approached down-sizing much less aggressively without regulatory stimulus. Since the record suggests a rapid pace of change with or without the EPCA and a reasonably sophis-ticated managerial response to the EPCA, there is little reason to believe that in the absence of government regulations GM's management would suddenly have been less sophisticated strategically and less responsible to environmental change. Stated more strongly, there is little reason to believe that the EPCA strengthened GM's hand in competing with the Japanese and several reasons to believe it weakened its position.

FORD MOTOR COMPANY

Ford, the number-two U.S. automobile producer, had long viewed itself as having to compete directly with GM. Ford had been a follower in styling but, recently, a leader in seeking out new product niches. Its strategy had been to occupy niches that it could exploit profitably before its competitors could move in. Thus Ford's product mix was augmented by specialty vehicles —for example, Mustangs, vans, and pickups—in addition to a full line of family cars. Ford had also concentrated on producing high-volume products. Small cars accounted for about 50 percent of Ford's sales versus 40 percent of Chevrolet's. While Ford had a great strength in small cars and specialty cars, it suffered from an overall weak mix, especially in relation to GM's middle-level Buick/Oldsmobile/Pontiac market. Despite strenuous efforts, Ford's return on investment and on sales continued to be, at best, 20 to 30 percent lower than GM's. The inability to develop a rich product mix and to lessen dependence on small cars put Ford in a weaker competitive position than GM long before the EPCA. Moreover, small cars are typically less profitable per year than larger cars, besides being more vulnerable to economic downturns.

Ostensibly, given Ford's small-car orientation, it ought to have been positioned favorably when energy prices rose in the early 1970s. Such was not the case, however, because CAFE standards coupled with gasoline price control made small-car lines even less profitable than they otherwise would have been.

Faced with these circumstances, Ford appears to have adapted its corporate strategy to the political imperatives of public policy. Ford began its down-sizing at the low end of its product line, down-sizing its full-size cars first in the 1979 model year—two years after GM. Apparently Ford's strategy was an attempt to protect its small-car share from imports while remaining ready to find a possible niche in positions that GM was vacating due to its down-sizing. In 1977 consumers still preferred larger cars, and regulated fuel prices reinforced this preference.

The cornerstone to the successful execution of the Ford strategy was the introduction of the Fairmont and Zephyr compacts. When they were introduced in 1977 they nearly doubled Ford's small-car mix to 38 percent of overall sales. They also helped Ford boost its U.S. market penetration to 24.4 percent, from the previous year's 22.9 percent. But Ford's sales gains were not without cost. Speaking to shareholders in May 1978, chairman Henry Ford II noted that "demand for a less profitable mix of vehicles" was partly to blame for the company's 23 percent decline in first-quarter earnings from its North American operation.[6]

After the Iranian revolution and the subsequent oil shortages, the market shifted dramatically toward smaller cars. GM was successful in convincing buyers that its down-size car lines were competitive with available large cars from Ford. Ford, the last firm to produce full-size cars—apparently an effort to exploit the competitive opportunities ostensibly created by regulation—was left in the uncomfortable position of trying to catch up with GM. Compounding Ford's adjustment problems were limitations in capital that could be spent on retooling. The lack of capital stemmed in part from large losses in its European operations that were unrelated to U.S. regulatory actions. However, Ford's lack of cash was clearly exacerbated by the lack of profitability of the small-car lines, again, a lack of profitability contributed to by CAFE standards and regulated gasoline prices. Ford's shortage of capital made the simultaneous deferral of large costs, elimination of down-sizing for large vehicles, and generation of cash by milking the existing car lines extremely attractive.

Unfortunately, the strategy was vulnerable to rapidly escalating gasoline prices and oil price decontrol, both of which occurred. In other words, the Ford strategy of being the last to exit the large-car market was ideal in a world of energy price and regulatory consistency but was highly vulnerable to changes in either. Ford's decisions regarding the introduction of new products and its limited capital have taken its toll. It is difficult not to see regulation and the specific strategic response it seems to have encouraged as playing at least a strong contributory role in the firm's subsequent financial difficulties.

CHRYSLER CORPORATION

For many decades Chrysler had been the smallest of the three major full-line domestic producers. There was a consistently lower level of repeat purchasers of Chrysler products compared with Ford or GM, at least partly as a result of a deteriorating reputation for reliability. Chrysler had in the past depended on a reputation for engineering excellence to sell cars. Despite its lack of resources in comparison to its competition, in the late 1970s Chrysler product policy hinged on a strong belief that it had to continue producing a full line of cars to remain competitive. Faced with GM's dominance in full-size cars, Chrysler had always suffered from a weak sales mix. Compact cars, less profitable than larger ones because they had lower margins and less potential for optional equipment, accounted for almost a third of Chrysler's production. Consequently, when a strong market for large cars emerged around 1977—in large part as a result of regulatory action shielding consumers from high gasoline prices—Chrysler's full-line strategy served an important purpose; the large cars would presumably generate cash, which could then be plowed into the financing of downsizing projects.

Chrysler's effort to maintain its presence in the large-car market was not without its costs. The allocation of scarce capital to down-sizing large cars meant other investments had to be forgone. In particular, Chrysler chose not to produce all the engines for the Omni/Horizon line but to purchase some from outside suppliers. Unfortunately, however, just as Chrysler was strengthening the top of its line and not investing in small-engine production, consumers reacted to the Iranian oil shocks by swarming to the smaller cars. The Chrysler Omni/Horizon product lines were able to benefit from the radical change in consumer preference on a vehicle volume basis, but only to a limited degree on a total profitability basis, given the lack of vertical integration. Chrysler's wise (in hindsight) move to develop the Omni/Horizon subcompacts was undercut by *Consumer Reports'* determination that the model's safety standards were unacceptable; it is also true that its apparent hedging strategy, in which scarce capital was committed to large cars instead of vertical integration into smaller-engine production— a strategy adopted in the face of energy policy constraints— seems to have played a serious role in undermining the profitability of these lines.

In retrospect, Chrysler's strategic commitment in 1977 to large cars was ill-timed. Without the benefit of hindsight, however, it is not at all obvious that such a strategy was ill-conceived. After all, there were strong regulatory pressures for the strategy Chrysler actually pursued.

The Lessons

The first and most fundamental conclusion from this discussion is also the most obvious: regulations and public policy can be expected to differ in their competitive impacts depending on the strategic responses and initial strategic positions of individual competitors within an industry. In all three cases, the impact of government policy on domestic auto producers was shaped in large part by the corporate strategies that were in place at the time these public policies were initiated.

The second lesson is that it is especially dangerous to assess the strategic business consequences of public actions in hindsight. Because the automobile market did eventually turn to small, fuel-efficient cars, it may be presumed that a federal policy which ostensibly encouraged such a shift actually complemented the true long-run strategic interests of domestic producers. The danger stems from the failure to assess strategic consequences from the forward-looking perspective in which such decisions are actually made.

The federal government's energy policy toward the automobile, when viewed from the competitive perspective of U.S. producers, lacked coherence; its effort to encourage fuel economy while keeping gasoline prices low was doomed from the start. The policy lacked continuity. The dramatic change in policy after the Iranian revolution undermined all the strategic commitments firms had made to the earlier policy. Moreover, to the extent that it complemented the strategic interests of any particular producers—and the Iron Law says that some competitor will always gain—the winners appear to have been foreign producers whose long-term strategies were directly complemented by federal policy.

Auto Import Restraints

Just as fuel economy regulations varied in their competitive implications for domestic producers depending on the strategies, so too do the competitive impacts of automobile import restraint policies vary.[7]

Ostensibly, a domestic policy of restraining auto imports would be beneficial to all U.S. producers. Yet while this may be the case in the short run, it need not be the case in the long run, because of strategic adaptations induced by the regulatory action. Long-term strategic adaptations of trade restraint can have markedly different impacts on different domestic firms.

In 1980 U.S. automakers and the United Auto Workers, hit by a combination of recession in the domestic economy and the gasoline price increases of 1979, began to exert political pressure for import restrictions. The recession reduced total car sales in the United States, from a high of 11.3 million vehicles in 1978 to less than 9 million per year in both 1980 and 1981. At the same time, gasoline price increases caused consumers to shift to smaller, more fuel-efficient models. The import share of the U.S. new car market jumped to approximately 27 percent in 1980 and remained at that level throughout 1981: Japanese producers captured most of the import gains because they offered more small-car models and because their lower production costs allowed them to sell high-quality vehicles at low to moderate prices. Sales of U.S.-made cars plummeted to a nineteen-year low and domestic manufacturers experienced record losses at a time when they were trying to retool to meet the demand for small cars and intensified foreign competition. In March 1981 the Japanese government, acting under strong pressure from the Reagan Administration and Congress, announced that it would limit the number of automobiles shipped to the United States for two years beginning in April 1981; further restrictive measures were possible, and were adopted, in later years.

The short-run advantage of such a policy to domestic auto producers was obvious. With decreased Japanese import penetration, automobile prices would stabilize or rise, sale volumes would increase, as would profits. But these short-term gains were not without their long-term costs, which stemmed from the strategic adaptation a policy of import restraint would be expected to induce in Japanese competitive behavior.

Given the fact that regulations restricted the number of vehicles the Japanese could ship into the United States, the restraints provided a strong incentive for Japanese car producers to upgrade the quality of the product lines they export and to relocate their manufacturing plant to the United States. Despite the fact the trade restraint would presumably be temporary, past experience suggested that once an original period of restraint was in place, it tended to be prolonged through one variant or another. This was certainly the case in the steel and textile industries, for example.

There was no reason why Japanese producers should anticipate an end to a policy of auto import restraint. Consequently, one would expect Japanese automakers, constrained in production volume, to seek higher revenues through product upgrading. In addition, if import restraints reduced the overall growth of the Japanese automobile industry, producers might have trouble holding down their labor costs, given the long-time practice of expanding the labor force by recruiting untrained and low-paid high school graduates. One informal industry estimate suggests that a slowdown in the growth of the Japanese auto industry would add 5 percent annually to the unit labor cost. Such a cost change would strengthen the incentive to seek higher-margin segments of the automobile market in an effort to become relatively less dependent on volume economies for competitive success.

And finally, concerns for customer loyalty might also strengthen incentives for the Japanese to shift into higher-margin segments. As is well known within the auto industry, once a company sells a customer a vehicle, it has a good chance of selling him or her another one. Thus consumer loyalty patterns would tend to perpetuate any short-term shift in vehicle mix created by even a temporary policy of trade restraint.

There is strong evidence that Japanese producers have accelerated their efforts to upgrade their product models since the imposition of trade restraint in April 1981. After that date, the average price paid for imported Japanese cars for the first time exceeded the average price of new domestic cars in the U.S. market. This historic shift was due partly to quota-inspired price hikes on existing models but also to substantial upgrading of imported car lines, particularly with the introduction of the 1982 models. The largest vehicle exporter, Toyota, which previously relied on the modest Corolla and Corona lines, completely revamped its higher-priced Celica line, with price hikes as high as 39 percent on some models. Second-ranked Nissan replaced its standard Datsun 510 with a more expensive Stanza and also introduced a new luxury line, the Maxima, with a list price of around $11,000. Equally significant, imported car models that had not yet been upgraded were being sold with more luxury accessories, such as air conditioning and power steering.

How were the U.S. manufacturers affected by these strategic changes?

FORD MOTOR COMPANY

The management of the Ford Motor Company was the most vocal advocate of trade restraint policy. Such a position was not surprising, given the company's short-term cash-flow needs—which would be eased substantially by a policy of import restraint—and apparent strategic commitment to smaller-scale automobile products. Given this strategic orientation in the long run and its cash-flow needs in the short run, Ford seems to have been positioned to participate substantially in the short-term gains due to trade restraint while suffering relatively little from the long-term losses attributable to the upgrading incentives facing the Japanese.

CHRYSLER CORPORATION

Chrysler was positioned much like Ford: near-term cash flow was extremely important and longer-term competitive success seemed to be in the lower-price, smaller-car market segments. Chrysler president Lee Iacocca, while less active in the early political negotiations for trade restraint due to Chrysler's tenuous financial relationship with the federal government, has subsequently become an outspoken advocate of trade restraint. Given his firm's corporate strategy, such a policy may well be warranted.

GENERAL MOTORS CORPORATION

GM, as the domestic firm with the largest market share, gains the most in short-term cash-flow generation from a policy of trade restraint—or at least is likely to—but is also most exposed to Japanese inroads in upscale product categories. Consider what happens every time a Japanese manufacturer sells a Maxima instead of a Corolla in the United States. GM is likely to suffer in the short run as the Maxima takes a sale away from the Oldsmobile line. It is true that the customer unable to buy the Corolla may well purchase a Chevrolet, but the increase in profits on the Chevrolet will not offset the loss in profit on the Oldsmobile. And GM continues to suffer in the long run as the Maxima owner repurchases a similar vehicle even after the period of trade restraint has expired. Not surprisingly, GM has not been an enthusiastic supporter of trade restraint.

Because GM is so large a factor in the U.S. automotive industry, it is highly likely that the net impact of automotive trade restraint, when viewed from the aggregate perspective of the U.S. industry, is negative if it is negative for GM. That is to say, the short-term benefits of cash flow generated by import restraint may well be worth less than the long-term cost of reduced profitability in upscale product categories as a result of the Japanese strategic response to import restriction.

The key competitive lesson, however, is not that the industry as a whole is better off or worse off due to import restraint, but rather that the implications for individual competitors differ and differ substantially depending on the corporate strategies in place once these trade restraint policies were initiated. Once again we see the Iron Law at work.

Conclusions

Public policies generally and government regulations in particular have a wide range of competitive consequences. Many of these consequences stem from the fact that public actions directly affect the costs of doing business. Moreover, these cost consequences are rarely uniform across competitors in an industry, and consequently the competitive impacts vary substantially among firms. Many other competitive consequences stem from regulatory change and its impact on the scale and timing of capacity decisions in industry. These cost and capacity impacts are among those most frequently receiving attention in political debates over government policy.

Still a third category of competitive impact exists: strategic impacts. Especially in markets where competition stresses product differentiation, the strategic consequences of public actions can be substantial and can be substantially greater than those otherwise attributed to cost or capacity impacts.

PART II

UNDERSTANDING GOVERNMENT WHEN COMPETITION MATTERS

Chapter 7

Understanding the Political and Regulatory Process

To appreciate adequately the competitive effects of government policy, it is essential to deal explicitly with the political nature of the policy process. Government policy is not imposed in a political vacuum. To the contrary, the formation of government policies affecting business must always be viewed as an interactive process in which all the actors are reasonably well-informed political as well as economic agents. It is necessary, therefore, to consider the nature of the political institutions creating the policies that have the variety of competitive effects described in the preceding chapters. If we understand how these institutions work, we might better understand the kinds of actions politically sophisticated economic actors will take in response to policy initiatives and, in turn, what the reaction of similarly sophisticated policy-making authorities is likely to be. While we will explore aspects of the regulatory process in greater detail in subsequent chapters, several attributes of the process are so important and recurring that it is useful to discuss them here.

Thinking in Terms of Equity

Perhaps the first thing to understand about the economic policy process is that it "thinks" in terms of what social scientists refer to as "equity" issues. That is to say, it is a political process that is very sensitive to the perceived fairness of any gains and losses to individuals and individual institutions affected by government action. Equity in this context does not necessarily mean either justice or equality in some egalitarian sense; as a practical matter, it often merely refers to the consequences of virtually any change from the status quo. It also refers to the practical reality that normative and judgmental issues of politics tend to be placed ahead of positive and substantive issues of technical or economic efficiency in most policy discussions. The consequence of this emphasis on equity may be greater justice or more nearly equal treatment of equals, but even when it is not, the political process tends to be sensitive to the implications of government policy for any particular affected group.

TANGIBLE LOSSES COUNT MORE THAN POTENTIAL GAINS

The concern for equity, it is worth stressing, tends to be asymmetrical. That is, the focus is usually on losses and not on gains. Thus a job lost in a closing manufacturing facility tends to be much more important than the job that might be gained by the increase in economic efficiency that such a plant closure may allow. Such asymmetry is obviously attractive politically: few beneficiaries of government action are likely to complain, and taking care of the inevitable losses due to public action is part of what a democratic society is all about. The fact that in the political eye the loss of an existing job, contract, or economic advantage cannot be easily offset by the gain from potential new opportunities is also evidence of a "bird in hand" notion that existing jobs, for example, are tangible, and future jobs merely prospects. This "bird in hand" notion recognizes that the individual who loses an existing job knows it, but the individual who fails to get a potential new job does not. In political accounting this is important arithmetic.

The "bird in the hand" notion makes it easy for executives in the steel industry, for example, to argue that steel imports cost jobs because employment is visibly declining in their sector. When others argue that import restraints will cost jobs elsewhere in the economy, the fact that these job losses are not visible detracts from the persuasiveness of the argument. Similarly, it is difficult to argue in favor of cutting an existing federal contract on the grounds that the freed revenue will either reduce the deficit or allow funding of other programs of equivalent or greater value to a representative's constituents: the existing contract is tangible; the alternative value is merely a promise.

Economists, of course, confront this tangibility issue constantly in economic policy arguments. The invisible hand of the market that economists champion is, as its name indicates, not easy to see working; in contrast, the visible hand of government is evidence of "something happening."

The concern for tangible losses versus potential gains has an important implication for political and regulatory processes: simply that these processes are likely to be biased toward the status quo because, as the Iron Law tells us, there will always be tangible losses due to policy intervention. Agents who enter the policy process after policy decisions have been made often see the benefit of the doubt given to the status quo. This places the burden of proof squarely on the intervenor. In contrast, agents who enter policy debates before decisions are made face a much more responsive audience.

The Equity versus Efficiency Debate

Political institutions intervene in the affairs of the market to achieve either—and often both—of two social objectives. First, intervention takes place to consciously change the distribution of economic outputs and costs across society. Examples of such "equity-motivated" intervention include enforcement of the government's nondiscrimination policies designed to redress years of hardship and injustice experienced by social minorities due to the collective prejudicial behavior of the majority; the imposition of windfall profits taxes in cases where profit levels are deemed "unjustly" high; and price controls in the so-called natural monopoly industries, such as electric utilities, where the absence of such controls might lead to monopolistic exploitation of consumers. In all these instances, governmental intervention is unapologetically political; that is, all parties recognize that government can and often does intervene in markets to achieve equity objectives. Many individuals question the wisdom of these interventions on both ideological and efficiency grounds, but few people deny the inherently normative and political nature of these equity-motivated policy actions.

Government also intervenes in markets to achieve economic efficiency. Indeed, one key element of the justification for regulation of natural monopolies is the fact that uncontrolled monopolies can undersupply and overprice products, with a consequent loss of economic efficiency. Similarly, governments intervene to protect the environment largely to achieve efficiency objectives, the argument being that unregulated markets produce an excessive and economically inefficient level of environmental degradation.

AN UNHELPFUL DISTINCTION

Ostensibly, the distinction between equity and efficiency provides a useful method for separating those forms of intervention that are "political," as equity interventions always are, from those that are "technical," as interventions to achieve efficiency goals are often presumed to be. In the classroom, the distinction permits a clear and analytically important intellectual distinction to be made. But in practice, the dichotomy is not all that helpful. As we have seen, the Iron Law of Public Policy applies to *all* regulatory interventions, no matter what their rationale: all policies create winners and losers. There is no exception in the Iron Law for efficiency-motivated policies.

Because there are always winners and losers and because any judgment of the equity of these gains and losses is always normative, it necessarily follows that all government interventions into the marketplace are inherently political in nature. This, of course, is not news to any seasoned participant in the regulatory process. Its importance, however, lies not in this practical political observation but rather in the fact that conceptually as well as practically it is not possible to avoid the political nature of economic policy actions. The point is worth stressing because proposals for reforming government policy frequently state as a goal the elimination of politics from the regulatory process. A practical individual would observe that such isolation from politics is impossible; a democratic theorist would observe that such a goal is undesirable.

This is not to say, of course, that it is never practically possible or theoretically desirable to reform business/government relationships to shield them from certain political forces. To the contrary, the very nature of most institutional reform is to shape the manner in which political forces are expressed, managed, and reconciled.

The economist's usual approach to avoiding the inherently normative aspect of all regulatory interventions is to acknowledge that successful efficiency-motivated intervention has the redeeming virtue of increasing the size of the economic pie available and thus permits all individuals, at least conceptually, to get a bigger piece. Of course, the necessary allocation process to ensure that all .individuals do get larger pieces is itself a political question. There is, in other words, no escaping the inherently political nature of microeconomic policy.

The Process Responds

Because the policy process is so concerned—and legitimately so —with the equity implications of public action, the process itself ends up taking on two additional characteristics. The first is that policy administration proves to be very responsive to the microlevel impacts of its own actions. Aggrieved individuals who seek redress of "wrongs" perpetrated on them by government are often successful in dealing directly with regulatory and political officials. Indeed, formal political intervention is frequently not even necessary because program administrators are aware that their own failure to respond to microlevel impacts will elicit some form of political reaction, and they take action to avoid this outcome. In preceding chapters we have seen this responsiveness—first to George Lockwood and his tiny operation at the Monterey Abalone Farms and then to the business interests in the fluorocarbon controversy, leaded gasoline debate, and so forth. For all the popular criticism of the federal government for alleged bureaucratic lack of responsiveness, a closer look—at least in the area of business/government relationships—suggests that it is actually much more responsive than we expect.

THE PROCESS MANAGES EQUITY

The second attribute of a process preoccupied with equity is that it creates a willingness among administrators and legislators to manage the instruments of policy to achieve conscious equity objectives. The willingness to pursue equity goals aggressively does not imply a complementary willingness to acknowledge explicitly this political pursuit. To the contrary, the political and regulatory process thrives on so-called objective and technical analysis and casts a high percentage of all policy questions in efficiency terms—whatever their real motives. It is often very difficult to determine just what it is that motivates particular regulatory actions since the efficiency agenda is visible while the equity agenda often is not.

Equity versus Efficiency: Which Is It?

An example illustrates that the problem of disentangling a policy maker's true goals is not merely a consequence of political obfuscation and lack of candor; rather, it is a fundamental consequence of the Iron Law that results in winners and losers from all policy transactions.

At the beginning of his first term as governor of Massachusetts, Michael Dukakis appointed young, aggressive, and reform-minded James Stone as State Insurance Commissioner. With automobile insurance rates among the highest in the nation, few Massachusetts residents would deny the need for reform.[1]

Stone possessed a Ph.D. in economics from Harvard and, not surprisingly, was interested in an economically efficient structure for insurance regulation in the state. His proposed reforms made a good deal of sense from strictly an economic standpoint. By basing rates on driver experience, for example, rather than sex, age, and geography, he was responding to longstanding needs to base auto insurance rates on more objective and economically efficient behavioral criteria. He was also aware of political realities. The efficiency motive notwithstanding, the principal impact of these reforms related to their consequences for equity. Some individuals in the state saw their insurance bills swing by sums exceeding seven hundred dollars per year due to these "technical" and efficiency-oriented reforms.[2]

There is no doubt that political concerns for equity influenced these deliberations. Indeed, how could they not? After all, the change in insurance bills for many individuals exceeded their total income tax payments to the Commonwealth. If so large a redistribution of income were to be considered through tax policy, no one would question the political legitimacy—indeed, the constitutional necessity—of addressing the equity issues explicitly, thoughtfully, and thoroughly. Such an examination would not be limited to technical inputs from tax professionals but would necessitate inputs from throughout the political system. Moreover, the resulting decisions would not be made in a regulatory proceeding by an appointed official like Stone but in a legislative setting by elected public officials. The procedural tests of accountability would not be merely administrative but constitutional.

The problem is that in a regulatory process where the inefficiencies are so great and the equity consequences of reform so dramatic, it is difficult to disentangle the roles that efficiency and equity play. The distinction is important, however, because there is no doubt that insurance reform was not something to be left strictly to the technically sophisticated actuaries and economists—society's stake was simply too great. On the other hand, the regulatory process is designed to handle technical detail and communicate in technical terms. As such, it often obscures the political discussion from the public's eye while allowing its actors to stake out major political positions in the name of some allegedly objective concept of efficiency. After all, when issues of equity are discussed using the technical jargon of insurance underwriters and statisticians, it is not easy for the average citizen to follow what is really being said. Yet, throughout these policy debates, seemingly technical decisions were being made that had major impacts on both insurance consumers and insurance providers.

POLICY IN A FOREIGN LANGUAGE

Regulatory proceedings of the type just described tend to be conducted in the foreign language of technical jargon. Often the real issues are not "technical" at all. Because arcane technical terms are used and because efficiency is a "good thing," it is not always necessary for regulatory proceedings to ever address equity issues explicitly, despite the fact that they are often implicitly preoccupied with them. Thus, for example, hearings over telephone access charges stressed the efficiency consequences of such charges, while the real agenda related to who pays what. The public, while legitimately interested in both the equity and efficiency questions, struggled to understand what an access charge was in the first place, never mind its merits and demerits. Similarly, a regulated public utility company will ask for "construction-work-in-progress"—so-called CWIP—to be included in the rate base or push for accelerated capital recovery to lower total costs or facilitate technological change. These legitimate efficiency-oriented questions have major equity implications in both the political sense of fairness and the private financial sense of capital value that are often the true object of concern. Accelerated capital recovery, for example, may well give a regulated firm the wherewithal to finance new technology, but it also serves the financial interests of stockholders. The average citizen, however, can hardly be expected to know what construction-work-in-progress is, how a rate base is defined, or whether something as technically complicated as accelerated capital recovery will have any good effect at all.

Equity in Efficiency's Clothing

The Iron Law tells us that all government actions create winners and losers. Thus it is possible to achieve equity goals through the use of policies designed ostensibly for economic efficiency. There is no need to raise the political red flag of equity directly if the same political goal can be achieved in the guise of efficiency. Accordingly, there is a strong tendency to dress equity issues in efficiency's clothing. Sorting out the real equity/efficiency trade-offs that are at the heart of public policy making thus becomes very difficult in an institutional process that often uses technical language to shield itself from charges of political motivation.

Process versus Outcome

When the natural political concern for equity is combined with the fact that all regulatory actions, whatever their motivation, create winners and losers, it is not really surprising that the policy process is often preoccupied with equity issues. What is perhaps less obvious is that political actors are sometimes more concerned with the equity implications associated with the *process* of intervention itself than with the individual rules that constitute the *outcome* of intervention.

It is important to stress that in the United States, political system fairness and equity are not always defined by outcome. To the contrary, there is a long political tradition that defines fairness in terms of "due process." Thus, as a nation, we do not guarantee individuals "equal achievement" but "equal opportunity." The distinction is between procedure and outcome.

The importance of procedure is magnified even further once we recognize that there is likely to be no "steady-state" in a world in which there are always winners and losers due to government intervention and in which the extent of gains and losses is measured not only by comparison with the status quo but by comparison to expectations as to what gains and losses would be under alternative policy regimes. It is not surprising, therefore, that in this institutional context, rules and regulations can be expected to change and evolve continually. It is *process,* as well as regulatory *outcome,* to which competitors must devote their attention.

Change Creates Political Value

Regulatory change is thus the currency in which government policy makers conduct business. Change, not stability, creates political power. For one thing, it creates winners and losers, and thus political potency, through the operation of the Iron Law. Without winners to appeal to and losers to placate, there is no need for political action. Perhaps more important, because the valuation of these gains and losses is inherently normative, it provides legitimacy to political intervention, which, after all, is designed to handle such normative issues. Not surprisingly, with change creating both political power and the legitimacy to exercise it, the regulatory process is best thought of as a dynamic activity.

TOP DOWN VERSUS BOTTOM UP

To understand the dynamics of the regulatory process, it is useful to compare the organizational structures of public- and private-sector institutions. Corporate organizations are often hierarchical in structure—that is, formal, pyramidlike structures of decision making allow executives at the topmost levels to communicate and enforce decisions downward through the corporate structure.

While this hierarchical nature can be exaggerated and clearly varies from firm to firm, there remains nonetheless a strong tendency in many corporations for strategic direction, entrepreneurial initiatives, and major decisions to come from the top. Indeed, even in those organizations that do not operate this way, the formal choice of an alternative organizational design was often the product of an earlier strategic decision from the top.

In the public sector, bureaucratic initiative often moves in the other direction. One reason for this difference is that many top-level officials in government are appointed for very short stays in agencies that must deal regularly with considerable technical detail. Because the technical information is the responsibility of career civil service professionals, there is a clear tendency for most information and much initiative to percolate up through the system. This is especially the case in regulatory agencies where arcane facts are often necessary to justify policy actions.

It is, of course, possible to overstate the bottom-up organizational tendency in the public sector. There are many stories of new senior political appointees coming in to federal agencies and reshaping them top-down. But again, as a general observation, the bottom-up versus top-down distinction is a useful one.

Former Secretary of the Treasury Donald Regan provides at least casual evidence of this distinction. After a very successful career as head of Merrill Lynch, Regan took over as Treasury secretary under President Reagan. After only a few months in office, he was quoted by the press as observing that the Treasury Department simply did not respond to directives from the top the way Merrill Lynch did. This was not so much a criticism of the Treasury bureaucracy as a recognition of the nature of government organizations, legislative constraints, congressional oversight, and the like.[3]

One consequence of these differing organizational forms is that high-level executives in the private sector often find themselves dealing with relatively low-level bureaucrats in the public sector; the social dynamics of their interaction can be important in determining how well the business/government relationship works. Often the interaction is negative when a senior executive, accustomed to working with others of equal rank, confronts a public-sector "functionary." The importance of unfamiliar rules and procedures of government process can become magnified when this apparent challenge to social status occurs.

The potential for counterproductive interaction due to these differing organizational forms is magnified by two other realities. For an individual enterprise, the indirect competitive effects of government action are often the primary focus of attention. Not so for the government agencies. An Environmental Protection Agency administrator who observes that a new rule will "only" cause one plant in one thousand to close has a very different view of this statistic than the manager of the one misfortunate plant. Seeing this statistic, the administrator's priorities are likely assigned to other issues and a relatively low-level staff person may have to deal with the exception. Moreover, given the agency's broader concern for the integrity of its overall environmental program, it is unlikely to be willing to conform policy to the needs of one individual firm.

From the firm's perspective, the EPA looks unresponsive, lacking in compassion, ignorant of economics, and even arrogant in relegating a firm's life or death to a low-level official. These conflicts will, of course, always exist in regulatory affairs, but dealing with them can be complicated by the differing nature of organizational structures in the public and private sectors.

The Business/Government Game

If business/government interaction is sometimes made more complicated by unfamiliar organizational structures, the interactive nature of the process also complicates things. The policy process is interactive in the sense that implicit and explicit political and normative considerations are relevant to the entire regulatory process, not merely the legislative stage of decision making, as many individuals unfamiliar with governmental processes sometimes believe. Indeed, it is useful to view the regulatory process as a game being played on successive playing fields.[4] This not-so-trivial pursuit begins in the broader body politic where issues are created and debated in the media and other political forums. The game then moves to the legislative arena. Once legislation is passed, it must be administered, and the playing field shifts once again. From time to time the game moves into the courts and even back to the media or the legislature. In each of these arenas the rules of the game differ in their degree of formality and procedure. Yet each arena in its own way helps shape the pattern of winners and losers that policy continuously creates. While action passes from one arena to another, there is always the opportunity to turn back. To view the regulatory game as won or lost due to a single victory or defeat in any particular arena at any given time is to misunderstand the sophisticated, ongoing, and interactive nature of regulatory institutions.

Not only does the game shift from one playing field to another, but the players' strategies shift as well. In what sometimes appears as inconsistency, a firm might seek one action in the courts, for example, while seeking the opposite action administratively. Often there is no contradiction at all, for as the game shifts from field to field, so do the rules and, thus, the interests of individual players.

An example involves the EPA and several pulp manufacturers in the Pacific Northwest.[5] The technical issue involved the right of several paper mills to discharge waste water out at sea where there was little, if any, environmental consequence. The competitive issues related to the fact that regulatory compliance costs to avoid such discharges could exceed forty dollars per ton for a product selling for only four to five times that amount. In the course of the debate over this issue, there were arguments that waste treatment would actually cause more environmental damage than it prevented because treatment would require the use of pollution-creating electricity, coal, and chemicals. According to this argument—which had considerable merit in the context in which it was applied—stringent pollution control was undesirable from both aggregate economic and ecological perspectives. Treatment, in other words, was allegedly inefficient no matter how high the value placed on cleanup.

One firm involved in the dispute, ITT-Rayonier, Inc., sued the EPA but was eventually compelled to spend millions in compliance. Yet, rather than forcing it to close, a competing firm in Ketchikan, Alaska, was given a nominal fine for noncompliance in return for a promise to install effluent control capacity. With a change in administration, there was a desire to make the EPA's regulations less onerous to business. EPA officials, therefore, looked at the possibility of invoking some variance procedures to keep the Ketchikan firm and any other ocean discharger from spending money to bring their facilities in compliance when so little environmental benefit was at stake.

Not surprisingly, having lost in the courts, ITT-Rayonier's management opposed the variance policy.

There was, of course, nothing inconsistent in this opposition. Having failed in their earlier argument in the courts that they should be exempted from compliance on efficiency grounds, ITT-Rayonier argued in the executive branch against variances on equity grounds. The efficiency arguments were as valid as before, but the change in the circumstances the firm confronted in the move from one arena to the other led to an understandable change in company position.

The ITT-Rayonier case reinforces an important point about the regulatory process: having once denied the firm a variance in one arena, a subsequent grant of the same variance in another arena was a quite different matter, at least from an equity standpoint. What would constitute a fair and efficient resolution of the subsequent variance requests was far from self-evident. The answer must be political.

Shortsighted Actors

This example illustrates how current decisions shape future options in important ways. The *sequence* of regulatory decision making matters. This important reality must be juxtaposed against an additional reality: many of the actors in the regulatory process tend to have a shortsighted view of regulation's consequences, a view that can materially influence the outcome of sequential policy deliberations, sometimes for the worse.

ELECTION CYCLES AND POLITICAL GEOGRAPHY

On the government's side, the myopia is often a product of short election cycles, which create the public-sector equivalent of management's preoccupation with the next quarter's operating statistics.

And the geographic organization of U.S. political institutions

reinforces this myopia, especially when policy losers are geographically concentrated and winners geographically dispersed.
It is sometimes difficult, for example, for responsible politicians
concerned with the plight of the U.S. steel industry to admit the
reality that they are primarily concerned with existing jobs. No
politician really wants to acknowledge that a revitalized steel
industry with the means and the incentive to invest in new
plant and equipment would not only employ fewer people than
are employed today but would likely locate these new investments—and the associated jobs—in geographic areas other than
those possessing steel mills now. While a highly unprofitable
steel industry would cause a politically unacceptable loss of
jobs in many political jurisdictions, this should be little solace
to steel producers seeking government help. After all, a highly
profitable industry could jeopardize those same jobs. Because of
its myopic concern for today's jobs in today's locations, the
regulatory process has a natural bias against both industry
growth and profitability when such changes mean a materially
restructured industry.

ALLEGIANCE TO PROFESSION

It is not only politicians who suffer from myopia. Regulatory
professionals often display a myopia of their own. Bureaucratic
professionals often display a great deference to the professional
fields they represent. It is, for example, very difficult for an
economist ever to argue in favor of trade restrictions and maintain professional standing. This kind of discipline-based bias
can often limit the economic policy options thoughtfully
reviewed.

BUDGETARY BIAS

Two other forms of myopia characterize the government's
side of the policy process. First, policy administrators, not unlike their private-sector counterparts, are concerned with the

budgetary implications of their own actions. Given the choice between regulatory actions that cost money "on budget" versus those with "off-budget" costs, there is a natural tendency to pursue the former in place of the latter. Indeed, Professor Lacy Glenn Thomas of the Columbia Business School, in a study of the Consumer Products Safety Commission, estimated that the commission was prepared to take actions that incurred up to ten dollars in costs for businesses and consumers if such efforts would save as little as one dollar in the commission's limited budget.[6]

This ten-to-one ratio may actually be conservative when compared to actions of other regulatory authorities. In the Commonwealth of Massachusetts, for example, the Department of Environmental Quality Engineering (DEQE) had an annual budget of $50,000 to enforce the fuel use provisions of the Clean Air Act. With funds so limited, the agency did the only logical thing. It identified the less than one dozen fuel oil distributors in the state and mandated that they sell only those fuels with a sulfur content which would allow the hundreds of users in the Commonwealth to meet the standards on the atmospherically worst days of the year. This "lowest-common-denominator" approach was extremely costly to industry, for most of the time firms were compelled to burn expensive oil that was not needed for environmental protection.

Anthony Cortese, the DEQE's administrator, sought and eventually won $400,000 in additional funding for this program. With added resources, it was no longer necessary to control the oil distributors by use of a single standard; rather, standards could vary from one part of the state to another by time of year depending on air quality needs. The resulting reduction in the state's oil bill was over $100 million annually.[7]

PREOCCUPATION WITH RISK

Still another form of myopia that characterizes regulators stems from their preoccupation with the risk of their own failure. Regulators, facing risk, tend to shed it—by reducing it, if possible, but also by shifting it to someone else. It is the latter tendency that needs attention.

Consider the case of a Massachusetts state official responsible for pesticides. The issue involved a pesticide of very limited use, but on the EPA's list of potentially dangerous chemicals. The technical analysis of this chemical showed that even its proper use involved a health risk; its unauthorized risk constituted an even greater danger. Since this chemical was readily available in nearby New Hampshire and there was no effective alternative to its use in those applications where it was appropriate, the analyst concluded that Massachusetts residents would likely face less risk from authorized versus unauthorized use. The policy recommendation, however, was to ban the chemical on the grounds that if its authorized use did subsequently create a problem, the agency would be blamed; but if the chemical had been banned and the hazard occurred, the agency could point to the wisdom of its ban. Thus the official advocated a ban in full knowledge that such a ban might be more dangerous than controlled use; it was merely less risky bureaucratically.

The pressure for bureaucrats to shed risk is by no means irrational. Indeed, one other Massachusetts official responsible for the licensing of hazardous waste disposal described the following dilemma to me. If he licensed the disposal of hazardous waste, he faced the wrath of environmentalists and local citizens groups, but at least he knew who disposed how much of what waste and where they put it. If he denied permits, the wastes would still be disposed of in some manner—illegally and, worse still, unknown to him. While he preferred the licensing alternative, he risked being fired from his position for "going easy on polluters." This official, unlike his counterpart in the pesticides case, took the risk, with its associated implications for his professional and political advancement.

COMPETITIVE MYOPIA

Managers of regulated firms share their own sources of myopia. Any changes in the rules of the game can be expected to make some of their own professional capabilities obsolete, for example. Historically, fewer tasks have been more complicated than figuring out regulated transportation tariffs. Indeed, traffic managers made an art of the process. When regulatory reform promised to make some of the old systems obsolete, many of these same traffic managers did not applaud the resulting reduction in freight costs for their employers but decried the obsolescence of their highly specialized skills.

Moreover, regulatory change often means short periods of considerable uncertainty with attendant vulnerability of near-term profits. These characteristics combine to make the status quo particularly attractive to many managers in the private sector, even though the longer-term economic interests of the enterprises that employ them may be better served by regulatory change. It is thus interesting to observe that strong competitors under regulation who promise to be even stronger under deregulation are often unenthusiastic about regulatory reform because of the interim bout with uncertainty. At the other extreme, marginal firms are often afraid they might not survive a transition even though change may be their only long-run hope. With the strongest and the weakest competitors both opposing regulatory change, it is easy to see why industry support for regulatory reform can be so slow in coming.

Managers of regulated firms also tend to be myopic when it comes to understanding the dynamic competitive effects of government action. For example, a group of soft-drink bottlers were concerned about a Federal Trade Commission (FTC) ruling undermining the restrictions on exclusive territorial franchises that had been important to this industry for decades. The FTC proposed to change the rules to increase competition and thus lower prices to consumers. To overturn this ruling required congressional intervention. These bottlers fought this legislative battle and "won" in the sense that they successfully reestablished the status quo ante.[8] As a practical matter, these same bottlers likely lost, however, for they failed to ask who would win or lose with the FTC's rule. A competitive analysis might have shown that the likely winners were large, well-capitalized, and sophisticated bottlers—just the group opposing change.

Conclusion

Numerous books have been written on the political and regulatory process. The subject remains fascinating to students of management, politics, economics, and psychology. This is itself an important fact, for it reveals the complexity and mystery that surrounds the workings of regulatory institutions. The process is not easily understood, and any simplistic characterization is likely to be misleading.

There are, however, some attributes of the regulatory process that seem to recur with some regularity. A better understanding of these aspects should be useful to actors trying to figure out just how these obscure processes operate.

We have seen that one major characteristic of regulatory processes is that they are concerned with equity; that equity depends on both the fairness of the regulatory process as well as outcome; and that the ability to create and respond to equity issues is a potent political and bureaucratic instrument.

We have seen that the various actors in the political arena not only have conflicting interests, but they often have a myopic understanding of these interests. This shortsightedness greatly complicates a system where the competition of informed self-interests is intended to yield the social optimum.

And we have seen the political and regulatory process as a game, albeit a serious one. As in any game, changes in the rules most upset those players who have developed skills compatible with the old rules.

The game involves risk. With a public preoccupation with accountability, especially among its public managers, there is a strong tendency for the various players to shed risk—sometimes by taking actions to lower it, and sometimes by shifting potential blame to others in what might be considered the bureaucratic analogue to the childhood game of "hot potato."

Each of these attributes of the regulatory system has implications for competition. It is, in other words, impossible to understand competition when government matters without understanding the dynamic processes of regulatory institutions.

Chapter 8

Coping with Public Policy:

The Naïve Response

The preceding chapters have described the various ways in which government regulatory decisions shape competitive behavior. We have seen that the indirect and typically unintended consequences of government intervention in markets have tended to dominate the direct consequences of public regulation. We have seen that in all cases, whenever government intervenes and for whatever objective, there are winners and losers within the affected industrial sector. And finally, we have seen that the political and regulatory process is itself critical to understanding the competitive effects of public policy, for this process tends to be at least as interested in issues of equity as it is in efficiency and for various institutional reasons can be myopic when it comes to evaluating the long-term economic consequences of public policy.

It is this competitive and institutional environment in which managers must conduct their daily business affairs. But these affairs necessarily entail frequent contacts with public, political, and regulatory authorities. This chapter and the next two describe the types of responses that managers in the private sector might make to the competitive consequences of public action.

The discussion is divided into three parts, reflecting a fundamental difference between the initial response of managers to
dealings with the public sector and their subsequent responses.
Because these initial responses tend to be naïve, while subsequent responses tend to be far more sophisticated, it is useful
to describe them separately. This chapter describes the naïve
response to government policy and offers explanations about
why such responses take place. Chapter 9 examines in detail the
sophisticated response of a single firm to its political and regulatory environment. And chapter 10 generalizes from this experience and offers suggestions on how managers can best organize the business/government relationship within the firm to
achieve economic and political success.

The Naïve Response

A manager's initial response to governmental policy is often
naïve—as one might expect from an unfamiliar encounter. By
identifying the characteristics of this response, it should be
possible for others to move more quickly to sophisticated dealings with political and regulatory agencies. While there is some
danger in overgeneralizing from the experience of others, and
critics might suggest that the following categorization is unduly
stereotypical, it is useful nonetheless to consider the characteristics of the naïve business response to public economic action.

THE RESPONSE IS OFTEN IDEOLOGICAL

The first and perhaps the most obvious characteristic of the
naïve response of management to government policy is that it
tends to be ideological. That is to say, management's first reaction, especially to the adverse consequences of regulation or
government intervention, tends to be a principled one and not
an economic one. Intervention is "bad" for one reason or an-

other; interference in markets is "un-American" or otherwise undesirable; "government authorities do not understand the role business plays in society"; and the like.

While ideology obviously has an important role to play in any political process, in dealings between business and government an ideological response that has been arrived at narrowly or hastily tends to be counterproductive. For one thing, ideological responses to regulatory problems can obscure the underlying political legitimacy of the issues that government policy makers are attempting to address. An understanding of the fundamental political underpinnings of any call for regulatory intervention is essential to coping with the problem. It is not enough to dismiss calls for governmental action merely because one disagrees with them on ideological grounds.

Consider the growing public concern nationwide for the problems of solid waste disposal and the consequent initiatives in several state legislatures to impose restrictions on the disposal of soft-drink containers. These containers are one of the largest and most rapidly growing component of the nation's solid waste and litter stream. There is no doubt that there are complex technological questions as to what constitutes the best way of dealing with this problem. Should, for example, the nation revert to the use of reusable containers? Is it preferable to use one-way containers that can be recycled in one form or another? Is it better to have a mandatory return-deposit system or to hire individuals to pick up soft-drink litter from the highways? Is it a good idea for the government to intervene in markets such as this to bring about any of these outcomes? In other words, a range of both technological and ideological questions have to be addressed in dealing with this issue.

It is also true, however, that the soft-drink container problem is not strictly an interest of some liberal ideological fringe. As the president of the National Soft Drink Association expressed it, the concern for soft-drink container disposal is not a consequence of the "bird and bunny people" picketing various governmental and business establishments; rather the ultimate political legitimacy that makes this issue a public concern is created when "the conservative Republican suburbanite curses the empty soda can on his front lawn while doing his Saturday chore of lawn mowing." This same individual also noted that the political legitimacy of this issue notwithstanding, management in the soft-drink industry at virtually all levels had opposed not only action to address this waste disposal problem but even study of the issue for almost twenty years, on grounds that were largely ideological. During this twenty-year period of denial, some eleven individual states enacted restrictive container regulation.[1]

The mere fact that the "conservative Republican suburbanite" might not advocate the same solution to the litter problem as the "bird and bunny people" is, in many ways, of little consequence: both recognized a problem and that recognition— not an agreement on remedy—was the source of legitimacy for a political debate and, conceivably, a political solution.

In another example, critics of the auto industry for many years argued that auto manufacturers' disregard for environmental and safety issues represented antisocial behavior. Whether such was the case or not is for others to decide; it is now generally agreed, however, that the initial ideological reactions of the auto industry to the first public discussions of environmental and safety questions were counterproductive. Indeed, it is hard to conceive of any sophisticated corporation today repeating the actions of General Motors in 1960 when it hired a private detective to monitor the personal affairs of Ralph Nader in an attempt to undermine and discredit the safety campaign that he was advancing.[2]

The naïve perception that important public policy recommendations result solely from the ideological fervor of zealots is one of the most frequent "early mistakes" business managers make when confronting regulatory intervention. Whatever one may think of his politics and methods, Ralph Nader is as successful as he is by touching political nerves. In the absence of an underlying public concern for the issues he addresses, there is very little that an activist, even one with the skills and dedication of Ralph Nader, can accomplish.

Managers in the private sector often miss this important reality despite being comfortable with an analogous process of their own: advertising. Virtually all sophisticated marketers know that it is not possible to create a market for a product unless that product taps some unmet consumer need or interest. Sometimes these "needs" are whimsical and transitory, but in every case a product must ultimately touch some consumer interest—economic, physical, or psychological. In the same way, public policy "entrepreneurs" of the Ralph Nader variety succeed only when *they* tap some unmet public need.

The political process is fundamentally a process of compromise; positions based on principle are, virtually by definition, difficult to compromise. A politician's task is a difficult one. Numerous interests must be heard and balanced, many of them conflicting. In the absence of some flexibility, the task becomes impossible. When issues are presented as categorically right or wrong, it is easy for the entire political process to break down.

This is not to argue against principle but rather against too hasty an invocation of principle. Indeed, one of the primary virtues of the U.S. political system is that it is based on a relatively small number of basic principles embodied in the Constitution. Over the years the country has been highly successful in preventing the encumbrance of the Constitution with too many principles—thus current debates over balanced-budget amendments and women's rights. The simple fact of political reality is that when every political issue becomes an issue of principle, none is.

Still another danger in ideological responses is that corporations taking them run the risk not only of alienating important outside political forces but of alienating individuals within the firm who hold different points of view.

It is worth emphasizing that there is an increasing awareness that good management requires the sharing of corporate values. Thomas J. Peters and Robert H. Waterman emphasized this point in their best-selling *In Search of Excellence.* [3] Efforts to create a shared sense of corporate values can be substantially undermined if corporate ideological positions in political affairs are merely dictated by top management and are not the product of internal consensus building and value sharing.

And finally, the ideological response to regulation has as

perhaps its most serious negative consequence for business the fact that it diverts attention from a corporation's fundamental economic objectives and financial interests. This is not to say that a corporation's sole objective is financial. Rather it is to observe that society, through its system of laws, has created the corporate institution to advance certain public objectives in the area of economics. Corporate managers who divert their attention from the achievement of those objectives and focus instead on ideological questions can undermine the corporation in two dimensions: first, by consciously using it for purposes for which it *was not* designed; and second, for failing to pursue the objectives for which it *was* designed. Indeed, the use of the corporate pulpit to advance ideological positions not central to the corporation's social purpose might well be viewed as justification for further regulatory intervention.

THE RESPONSE IS OFTEN TECHNOCRATIC

It would, of course, be an overstatement to say that the initial response of management to regulatory intervention is always ideological; it is, however, frequently ideological and often naïvely so. When the initial response is not ideological, it often tends to be technocratic. The characteristic technocratic response to regulatory intervention is for management to call for the resolution of regulatory and public policy questions on economic, technological, or scientific bases rather than on the basis of political considerations. "Get the politics out of the regulatory process" is one of the most frequently heard statements in the naïve technocratic response to regulatory intervention in the marketplace.[4]

This response is naïve and typically ineffective because it does not address two fundamental realities. First, viewing regulatory issues as technocratic ignores those legitimate value-laden questions that do, in fact, have to be addressed in all regulatory proceedings. And second, as we have previously observed, whatever the rationale for regulatory intervention in the marketplace, such intervention always creates winners and losers. The existence of winners and losers imparts an inher-

ently normative characteristic to all policy interventions. That
is to say, economic and regulatory decisions are inherently and
legitimately political, not merely as a consequence of the workings of various bureaucratic institutions but because they represent societal decisions regarding the production of different
kinds of goods and the distribution of income and wealth
among individuals. A technocratic orientation tends to ignore
this fundamental political character.

THE RESPONSE IS OFTEN AN EXERCISE IN MIRROR IMAGING

A third characteristic of the naïve response of management
to regulation is that it often represents an exercise in "mirror
imaging"—implicitly assuming that characteristics of one's
own decision-making apparatus apply to the apparatus of those
with whom one is negotiating. The most frequent expression of
this temptation to mirror imaging in the domestic political context is the statement "We share the same objectives but merely
have different means of achieving them." In reality, it is most
often these allegedly "shared objectives" that are, in fact, the
points of contention.

In initial responses to governmental intervention in the marketplace, the mirror-imaging problem tends to manifest itself
by private-sector managers assuming incorrectly that the organizational structure which characterizes their own corporations also characterizes the organization of government. As
noted in chapter 7, many corporate structures are hierarchical
in nature. That is, they are top-down organizations in which
each successively higher level of management possesses some
considerable authority and control over lower levels of management. In such a hierarchical organizational environment, an
individual tends to have a higher probability of influencing the
organization the higher the level in the organizational structure
he or she gets. According to this line of reasoning, you have a
better chance of influencing the strategy of General Motors by
interacting with the chairman of the board than with a local
plant manager.

As discussed, governmental agencies are not always similarly organized, however. Indeed, many governmental bureaucracies are bottom-up organizations. Because so many high-level governmental officials are appointed, and appointed for short periods of time, it necessarily follows that administrative and organizational continuity comes not from high levels of management but from the permanent civil service. What this means in areas involving complex technological questions like health and safety regulation, for example, is that many issues and policy initiatives percolate up from the bottom of the system to the top. In such a bottom-up system, access to only the top without comparable access to the bottom of the organizational structure often reveals a sympathetic ear but little in the way of a substantive response.

In dealing with public authorities for the first time, managers familiar with the organizational hierarchy of corporations often try to establish contact at as high a level as possible. Thus a business executive with an environmental problem will eschew contact with the bureaucracy and instead try to contact the regional EPA administrator. Better still, in this view, contact the head of the EPA in Washington. Using this same line of reasoning, those with sufficient political clout deal with a congressional representative, a senator, or go directly to the president. What managers typically discover when they pursue this path is something of a "good news/bad news" joke: the good news is that it is far easier than they ever expected to make direct contact with the very highest levels of government officials. Having prided themselves on arranging a conversation with a U.S. senator, only then do they discover the bad news that the sympathetic ear of a senator does not, by itself, mean the resolution of their regulatory problem.

THE RESPONSE IS OFTEN REACTIVE AND AD HOC

A fourth characteristic of the naïve response to regulatory intervention is that it tends to be reactive and ad hoc. Of all the characteristics of the naïve response, this is probably the least avoidable because few managers, since they lack an obvious incentive to do so, are likely to pursue a program of preemptive regulatory action. But what the reactive position confronts is the reality of the Iron Law of Public Policy. Because all regulatory interventions create winners and losers, and because the political process is reasonably responsive to the individual concerns and interests of those who participate in that process, managements that react to government policy *after* actions have been taken confront entrenched interests from their own industry who are among the beneficiaries of the policy in place. These entrenched interests, of course, can create a political opposition with which management must contend.

A classic example of this phenomenon occurred in the natural gas industry. For years, natural gas wellhead prices had been subject to federal control. To cope with rising energy prices and declining supplies, federal regulators concocted an elaborate set of pricing rules. One of the consequences of these rules was that so-called new gas—gas discovered under certain conditions and after certain dates—carried a price far different from so-called old gas. (In fact, there were dozens of variations on old and new gas, but the simple distinction will suffice for illustration.) New gas could sell at a level several times higher than old gas. Moreover, because the supplies of old gas were relatively fixed, new gas, by definition, had to absorb most of the competitive forces placed on the gas industry. With so much gas subject to price regulation, these demands were substantial, since most rational consumers knew a good deal when they saw it and consumed large quantities of inexpensive gas. As a result, demand for gas was higher than it would have been in the absence of price controls. With all this pressure for added supply falling on new gas, its price was actually higher than it would otherwise have been in an unregulated market.

Enter decontrol advocates. The merits of their case notwithstanding, who were the principal protagonists? Why, the producers of new and old gas. Those firms owning old gas reserves wanted decontrol so that their gas prices would rise to market-clearing levels; owners of new gas opposed control because their prices would *fall* to market-clearing levels. And consumer groups, of course, were wary of decontrol.[5]

With consumer groups opposed to decontrol and business interests divided, it is little wonder that regulation has been so difficult to eliminate. But the key point is that the divided business interests were created by prior regulatory interventions. Prior intervention created entrenched interests whose political activities influenced subsequent policy debates. Such entrenched interests always exist, of course, thus the conclusion that proactive responses to regulatory intervention are preferred if creation of such opposition is to be avoided.

THE RESPONSE IS OFTEN BLIND TO COMPETITIVE REALITY

While it is hard to see how a firm's initial response to government intervention is likely to be anything but reactive, the fifth characteristic of the naïve response is avoidable. Managers confronting regulatory initiatives for the first time often become so occupied with the public purpose that regulation is intended to achieve that they fail to see the competitive relevance to the corporation of the public policy in question.

For example, during the 1970s there was great political concern for the consequences of rising utility prices for low-income families. As a result, there were numerous initiatives in state legislatures, some effective, some not, to impose so-called lifeline regulatory structures on public utilities. These lifeline rates were intended to ensure that low-income people had access, at some affordable cost, to the minimum level of electricity, natural gas, or telephone service that they might require.[6] The ideological response of most utility managements to these initiatives was expectedly negative. They argued that achievement of social welfare goals was a responsibility of the general public and not of individual utilities.

The merits or demerits of this argument notwithstanding, it is interesting to note what kinds of analyses some managers conducted in the face of these lifeline proposals. Typical analyses focused on what policy makers referred to as the "target efficiency" of lifeline initiatives. In welfare programs there is always a concern as to how well they achieve their original objectives. Thus, for example, from a public policy perspective it is important to know whether a lifeline electricity rate would *actually* help low-income electricity consumers. It might not if, for example, many low-income consumers used very little electricity and therefore would benefit little; it might not be helpful if they consumed substantially large amounts of electricity, in which case they would get the subsidy in one hand but have to pay it back out of the other in higher charges for consumption above the lifeline rate. Either case might negate any advantage resulting from some minimal level of electricity being provided at low cost. Or, alternatively, perhaps a reasonably large number of high-income persons also used only small amounts of electricity and would thus capture much of the benefit from a lifeline proposal. This might occur, for example, because high-income persons have second homes in which only small amounts of electric power are used or because they tend to install second telephone lines.

What was striking about these utility industry analyses was not that they constituted good or bad assessments of the benefits to society of lifeline rate proposals. Rather it was the extent to which they often ignored the functional and operating significance of these regulatory interventions to the utilities themselves. Lifeline rates, by changing the cost of initial levels of power consumption, for example, have implications for the level and pattern of energy use within the electric utility industry. Similarly, since any subsidy to low volumes of electricity must be made up by higher prices for larger users, it necessarily follows that such a lifeline structure affects marginal decision making in this industry. The implications for the pattern of demand, the consequent types of operating capacity that would be required, the financial implications of lifeline rate structures, and so forth, were too often ignored in the utilities' analyses.

This electric utility response was not an unusual one. In initial dealings with new forms of regulatory intervention, management often fails to see the functional and competitive implications of public policy and instead focuses on second-guessing the public purpose the policy was designed to achieve.

The Shoo-fly Mentality

If there is an overriding characteristic of the naïve response to regulatory interventions, it is that it typically reflects what might be called a "shoo-fly" approach to government. That is to say, many managers confronting political and regulatory intervention for the first time see it as an issue that will no longer bother them once they make it go away—once they swat the fly, they will no longer be pestered. Animals discovered the folly of this reasoning many millennia ago and evolved tails as permanent fixtures to address an unavoidable reality.

The failure of many business managers to appreciate that regulatory interventions are a pervasive characteristic of the business environment and that political and regulatory institutions are process- and not merely outcome-oriented contributes to this "shoo-fly" mentality. As subsequent discussion will reveal, sophisticated managers appreciate that government intervention is not a fly that can be swatted and thus eliminated but rather a reflection of constantly present and pervasive institutional forces with which they must reckon.

Chapter 9

Understanding versus

Influence:

The ECOL Experience

Chapter 8 described the naïve business responses to government regulation. Let us now consider the basic components of a sophisticated response.

The Sophisticated Response

1. Sophisticated responses tend not to be ideological.
2. Sophisticated responses do not confuse technical details with value-free, apolitical decision making.
3. Sophisticated responses treat regulatory organizations as they are, not as reflections of corporate hierarchy.
4. Sophisticated responses are proactive.
5. Sophisticated responses reflect a well-informed appreciation of the competitive implications of governmental intervention in competitive markets.

The following case study will show that perhaps the basic characteristic of the sophisticated business response to government policy is that it is predicated on a fundamental understanding of political and economic processes and not merely on an inflated self-assessment of the corporation's ability to influence that process.[1]

The Energy Corporation of Louisiana

The Energy Corporation of Louisiana (ECOL) was a joint venture of Northeast Petroleum Industries and Ingram Corporation. In late spring 1974 ECOL's top management was meeting to decide whether or not to exercise an option to purchase land for a new oil refinery to be constructed upstream from New Orleans. The planned 200,000-barrel-per-day facility would be the largest grass-roots refinery ever built in the United States and the first major U.S. refinery designed to maximize fuel oil production rather than gasoline. It would also be the first large-scale independent marketer to enter the domestic refining industry.

Design of the refinery and initial site preparation had begun a year earlier. Agreements on loans of up to $350 million were pending with a group of banks and other investors. ECOL partners were reviewing the refinery's potential profitability amid a climate of regulatory change in the petroleum industry. ECOL's management was concerned that the construction and working capital costs of the refinery, approximately $400 million, could cause the partners serious financial problems. They were also concerned that the uncertainty in the crude oil markets and energy regulation increased the risk of committing such large sums of money to an investment decision that could begin yielding profit in, at best, two to three years.

The economic attractiveness of so substantial an investment was far from apparent. Refinery utilization rates were then running at about 77 percent, although they had been running at much higher rates only a year earlier and numerous forecasters were predicting a refinery capacity shortage. Given ECOL's heavy burden of debt, its break-even level of operation was approximately 76 percent utilization. To be profitable, in other words, ECOL had to perform substantially better than the industry as a whole was doing at that time.

The prospect that it could outperform the industry seemed limited. ECOL did not command lower costs of operation than its larger competitors, although its management felt that the new facility would be at no substantial disadvantage on an operating cost basis. The real cost concern and resulting competitiveness of the facility depended on the price of crude oil to ECOL.

The Initial Regulatory Conditions

ECOL's management anticipated no difficulty in signing long-term contracts for crude at acceptable world oil prices. Northeast Petroleum and Ingram both had extensive experience in trading crude oil and refined products. There was a catch, however: due to crude oil price regulations, the imported crude oil that ECOL would use was selling at approximately $15 per barrel at the same time that price-regulated domestic crude oil was available to many of ECOL's competitors at approximately $5.25 per barrel.

As if this $10-per-barrel price disadvantage were not enough, various other regulatory factors influenced the cost of operating the proposed ECOL facility. For example, when ECOL shipped its product to markets in the Northeast, it would be subject to Jones Act shipping requirements, which mandate the transportation of products between U.S. ports on ships built in the United States and staffed by U.S. citizens. This would add an additional cost disadvantage to the ECOL facility of approximately 60 cents per barrel when compared to its offshore competition.

There were, however, other regulatory considerations that

might work to ECOL's advantage. For one thing, an established policy of the Nixon Administration was to support development of independent, onshore refinery capacity. Moreover, in January 1974 the ECOL partners had met with William Simon, head of what was soon to be called the Federal Energy Administration (FEA). Simon apparently expressed his enthusiasm for the ECOL project. What all this political support meant substantively was not clear, but presumably it represented a commitment of the national government to the survival of ECOL and refineries like it. More tangible evidence of this commitment was contained in a tariff policy that granted a five-year exemption from crude oil import fees to new domestic onshore refiners for 75 percent of their product volume. This tariff advantage would materially reduce the transportation disadvantage created by the Jones Act.

Still, when all was said and done, the various regulatory factors inhibiting the ECOL investment were substantial. Stated most directly, if ECOL were forced to operate under the conditions prevailing in May 1974, the new refinery facility would represent perhaps the highest cost refining capacity in an industry that was only operating at a 77 percent utilization rate.

Regulatory Changes

In the face of these seemingly overwhelming odds against financial success, ECOL management decided to go ahead with the refinery's construction and operation. During the ensuing two-and-a-half-year period of construction, changes in the rules and regulations that would affect the ECOL facility when construction was completed were mind-boggling. Management's decision and the complex strategy designed to implement it helps illustrate just what it means to have a sophisticated understanding of competition when government matters.

The first regulatory change helped make the decision to begin

construction look better than it had before. Shortly after
ECOL's management decided to go ahead with the investment,
FEA officials announced a policy of oil entitlements. This program required all refiners to purchase an "entitlement" whenever they purchased domestic oil. These entitlements were purchased from importers of crude oil who, for every barrel of oil
imported, were granted one entitlement to sell by the government. Sale of the entitlement effectively lowered the cost of
crude oil to importers of crude while purchase of the entitlement increased the cost for purchasers of domestic oil. Not
surprisingly, competitive market forces set the price of entitlements such that the prices of domestic and imported oil were
equated, thus having the intended effect that all crude oil, both
domestic and imported, was sold at the same price.

As a consequence of this regulatory action, ECOL found itself
not one of the highest- but potentially one of the lowest-cost
refiners in the business. The reason, of course, was the elimination of the $10-per-barrel price differential on imported oil.
While ECOL remained at a competitive transportation disadvantage regarding its offshore competitors, the offshore competitors, by virtue of their location, were not eligible for the
entitlements and consequently still had to pay the world's market clearing price of approximately $15 per barrel of crude oil.
Given the tariff advantage that accrued to new facilities, ECOL
would actually find itself at a modest positive advantage vis-a-
vis a number of its domestic competitors.

The ECOL Business Strategy

The decision by the FEA to create the entitlements program
confirmed the wisdom of ECOL's commitment to the new refinery. To see how wise, it is useful to consider in some detail the
nature of the regulations imposed by the FEA and the strategic
business decisions of ECOL's management.

We have already observed that the entitlements program itself served to make ECOL a potentially low-cost producer. A low-cost producer, in an unregulated environment, can expect to reap two benefits: first, low costs tend to assure a high rate of capacity utilization; and second, low costs tend to assure high profit margins. In a regulated market, however, in which prices are tied to costs, only the utilization advantage counts because margins are fixed.

In any event, ECOL's heavy commitment to debt financing *necessitated* a high rate of utilization to ensure adequate coverage of interest costs. Accordingly, ECOL had arranged for approximately 60 percent of its product to be sold on a long-term, cost-plus basis to various agents. These agents included the parent companies of the ECOL firm and Middle South Utilities, a major lender to the project itself.

The signing of long-term, cost-plus contracts had at least two effects besides ensuring a reasonable level of capacity utilization. First, they effectively eliminated any prospect of increasing profit margins. At the same time, however, by signing contracts that kept margins fixed, ECOL also would avoid accusations of "excess profits." With price controls in place and so much of the viability of this project riding on favorable regulatory treatment, such an approach had political as well as economic merit.

ECOL's cost-plus contracts actually were the source of competitive advantage in a price-regulated market. By virtue of selling products to their own distribution companies and their major lender on a cost-plus basis, the firm effectively reduced the cost basis on which these businesses competed in the markets in which they operated. A low-cost basis is extremely important in markets where regulated prices are pegged to costs. The reason for this is simply that when prices are based on cost, customers will turn first to those facilities with the lowest costs of production and give them the highest rates of utilization. By passing through ECOL's cost advantage, these downstream activities were positioned for a high rate of utilization in the marketplaces in which they operated.

Thus, through the strategy of high financial leverage and long-term, cost-plus contracts, ECOL's management successfully turned price controls to a substantial competitive advantage. It positioned the firm to compete not on the basis of profit margins per barrel but rather on the basis of the rate of utilization not only in the refinery itself but in its other lines of business. The creation of the entitlements program had complemented ECOL's competitive strategy very well.

The sophistication of the ECOL strategy was not limited to creating the means for sharing the advantages of the entitlements program throughout the distribution channel but was also reaped in other ways. For example, the ECOL refinery was technologically configured to take high-sulfur crude and produce low-sulfur residual fuel oil and unleaded gasoline. Markets for both products were growing in response to new environmental regulations on emissions from both industrial and automotive sources. Moreover, on the world market high-sulfur crude oil tended to sell at a slight discount in comparison with average crude sources. Since the entitlement program established prices on the basis of *average* costs of imported oil, and ECOL was in a position to import lower-than-average-cost oil, this created a further cost advantage for the ECOL investors.

More Changes in Rules

Of course, none of these supposed advantages would accrue to ECOL until the refinery was completed. But during the period of construction when these regulatory changes were put in place, subsequent rules changes created additional competitive impacts with consequent political responses. For example, an Amerada Hess facility in the Virgin Islands had benefited substantially from FEA's entitlements decision. Consequently, while the demand for oil was declining in the face of rapidly rising prices, Amerada Hess actually doubled its market share in the northeast part of the United States in approximately one year's time.

As a result of such developments, there were enormous pressures for regulatory change, particularly from offshore refiners. The FEA, of course, was responsive to the political pleadings of these refiners because they were offshore by geography only. Many were actually owned and operated by major domestic U.S. oil firms. The FEA attempted to respond to the political pressures created by the offshore refiners who were placed in such a substantially disadvantageous position by taking three actions.

First, the FEA created a program of so-called reverse entitlements. Under this program, residual fuel refined on the Gulf Coast but sold on the East Coast would not be eligible for entitlements. This policy change was in response to concerns of offshore producers who were not eligible for entitlements but who sold their product in the Northeast market. This ruling meant not only that ECOL's entitlements were drastically reduced, but also that ECOL would have less of a cost advantage to pass through in its cost-plus contracts. Even with reduced entitlements, however, ECOL would still have a cost advantage compared to offshore competitors, albeit one that was greatly reduced.

Second, the FEA granted entitlements to customers of offshore oil. One difficulty confronting the FEA was that it would not be politically acceptable to grant non-U.S. facilities entitlements to price-controlled domestic crude oil. The FEA's creative response to this problem was to grant entitlements instead to the customers of these offshore refineries. This had the same desirable outcome from the offshore refiners' perspective because it stimulated total demand for imported oil products and thus improved their profitability and utilization.

And third, FEA simultaneously announced a shift in pricing policy. It deregulated the price of residual fuel oil. Because the world price of residual fuel oil had actually been falling during this period, there were political pressures to deregulate its domestic price to take advantage of a short-term glut in supply.

ECOL's management was dissatisfied with these regulatory changes—particularly the reverse entitlement program—and had to decide what actions to take.

Complicating its decision was the entrance of Marathon Oil Company onto the scene. Marathon produced price-regulated domestic crude oil in excess of its own refinery capacity. Because this crude oil was price-controlled the firm was, in effect, compelled to sell much of its product at substantially less than its market-clearing price, with the advantage accruing to the refiners who purchased the oil. It was attractive, therefore, for Marathon to expand its refinery capacity and make better use of its own crude oil supplies. Consequently, Marathon Oil management approached ECOL management regarding the possible purchase of the refinery.

Still Another Decision

Given regulatory changes that affected their investment adversely and the interest of Marathon, ECOL managers faced a difficult choice. Should they pursue discussions of a sale or should they appeal to the FEA the regulatory decisions that adversely affected them?

ECOL's management chose to appeal the FEA decision. The FEA responded to ECOL's appeal in a way intended to help the refinery. FEA officials observed that the principal economic obstacle to ECOL's success was its high debt level and the consequent cash-flow needs in the early years of the refinery's operation. They saw as well that their decision to deregulate the price of residual fuel oil placed the net cash flow position of the ECOL refinery in some jeopardy. Consequently, the FEA offered ECOL's management the loan of entitlements, the sum of which when sold on the open market would produce enough cash to cover the requirements of the fledgling operation during its initial years of operation. Stated differently, the FEA regulators proposed to use their regulatory powers to finance the working capital requirements of the ECOL facility.

The Outcome

This decision was handed down on September 10, 1976, approximately three weeks before the refinery was scheduled to begin operation. Literally on the same day, ECOL's management contacted Marathon Oil Company. Marathon responded to the FEA's proposal with an offer that would yield ECOL a profit of approximately $116 million. The firm had successfully taken its original $20 million equity investment and turned it into over $100 million in less than twenty-eight months without ever having processed a barrel of crude oil.

On September 20, 1976, ECOL's management sold the facility to Marathon. The transaction was consummated so quickly in still one more response to government regulation. Marathon Oil wished to take advantage of the investment tax credit associated with ECOL investment, but to do so had to purchase it prior to its completion at the end of September.

The claims in the public press were that adverse decisions by federal regulators had driven ECOL out of business even before it had begun operation. In its most literal sense, these journalistic accounts were correct. After all, had FEA officials granted ECOL's management requests for more advantageous regulation, the company might well have operated the facility. In no real sense of the term, however, did the FEA's overall actions penalize ECOL. To the contrary, the FEA's actions had generally substantiated the wisdom of management's decision to commit itself to this refinery in the first place. The partners in the ECOL investment earned well over $100 million as a result of their willingness to take risks in a highly changing and uncertain regulatory climate.

Why ECOL Succeeded

Upon hearing the story of ECOL, many individuals are inclined to believe that either ECOL's management was lucky or it possessed some hidden political influence that it was able to utilize to its advantage. The managers may well have been lucky and they may well have had some degree of political influence. What is most impressive, however, in the ECOL story is not its owners' and managers' ability to influence the governmental process but rather their ability to understand both the political and the economic significance of the events shaping this industry.

Given the regulatory uncertainty that ECOL's management confronted in the spring of 1974, it would not have been surprising to see the volatility of regulation paralyze management decision making. This did not occur. ECOL's management saw the opportunity to take advantage of government regulation, political forces, and economic opportunities to advance their competitive interests.

As of May 1974 there was no entitlements program in place. It was not possible to predict at that time that an entitlements program of the precise configuration of the one created would be put in place. It was possible, however, to appreciate the political pressures that would exist for some program of crude oil price equalization. ECOL's management understood this political pressure and took appropriate competitive actions.

It was also apparent at this time of political and public concern for high profit margins within the oil industry that it would be extremely naïve for any new entrant into the oil industry to depend on high margins for survival. ECOL's management recognized this political pressure and chose to develop its refinery to compete on the basis of utilization, not margin. Given this commitment to competition on the basis of utilization, a high rate of debt financing was the logical strategic financial move, for only through leverage could fixed margins be translated into high returns on equity.

ECOL's management apparently understood the political pressures regulators confronted. Its decision to produce low-sulfur fuel and unleaded gasoline were clear attempts to exploit areas of growing demand in markets that were otherwise declining as a consequence of rapidly rising oil prices. Even its location in the U.S. Gulf represented a sophisticated political understanding of the kinds of pressures that confronted new entrants into this industry. Prior attempts by Northeast Petroleum and others to build refineries in the Northeast where environmental forces were strongly opposed to such construction had taught ECOL that a more favorable political climate was the place to go in committing such large funds.

In sum, whatever ECOL's management did to successfully influence the regulatory process to its advantage was substantially outweighed by its sophisticated understanding of how regulatory institutions and political pressures work in complex industrial settings. It recognized those forces and turned them to competitive advantage by adopting marketing, financing, operating, and locational strategies all designed to exploit the economic opportunities created by the pressures of the government's industrial policy toward the energy industry. Nothing in the story of ECOL suggests political intrigue, power politics, or other forms of antisocial behavior. To the contrary, through its sophisticated understanding of politics and economics and the way they are joined through regulatory institutions, ECOL's management not only achieved substantial personal profit but advanced the interest of public policy makers in expanding the onshore refinery capacity of nonmajor U.S. oil producers.

A Key Lesson

The ECOL story is impressive for it shows what sophisticated players in the regulatory arena can do to advance their corporate interests as well as public policy goals. The story also reveals just how entangled the process of political economy can become. Starting from an initial desire to protect consumers from rising oil prices, regulators created the need for an entitlements program, the circumstances leading to a reverse entitlements program, and subsequently the opportunity to engage in a loan of these regulation-created credits to ECOL to aid it with its working capital financing. The specific circumstances are peculiar to ECOL, but the lesson is relevant to all managers and public decision makers.

Chapter 10

Organizing for a Sophisticated Response

As we have seen, managers confronting government for the first time often suffer from institutional naïveté: they simply do not understand how the political and regulatory processes work. Worse still, they typically fail to perceive the business relevance of government policy. They tend to criticize and comment on market intervention as public policy, not as a business consideration. They are much too often more concerned about whether or not a particular public action agrees with their own political views than its implications for market share, capacity, or future operating decisions. But with experience, managers can become more sophisticated. Sophistication in this context means understanding the governmental process and utilizing it to advance the legitimate interests of enterprise in a socially responsible way.

Understanding the Process

There is no doubt that to cope successfully with government, it is first necessary to understand political and regulatory forces. This is, of course, much easier said than done. Indeed, numerous scholars have dedicated their careers to developing this understanding. While, on balance, there is probably more that we do not know about regulatory institutions than things we do know, here are some rules managers can follow in trying to understand the way government regulates business:

1. Pay attention to issues of prelegislative political legitimacy.
2. Learn how the legislative process works.
3. Pay close attention to the process of policy administration.
4. Systematically examine the competitive implications of government action.
5. Look for ways to use government regulation as a competitive weapon.

PAY ATTENTION TO ISSUES OF PRELEGISLATIVE–POLITICAL LEGITIMACY

The first rule is to pay close attention to issues of political legitimacy. As noted earlier, political legitimacy is not a particular ideology, nor a matter of right or wrong. It is what a large part of the body politic accepts as an issue appropriate to discuss in the political process. A manager need not agree with a particular political position to understand the reasoning of those who do.

As a practical matter, it is difficult to define the concept of political legitimacy. This lack of precision merely serves to emphasize that the interpretation of legitimacy is highly judgmental. Just as a sophisticated marketer has to develop an intuitive feel for the interests of consumers by being "close to the customer," so too must managers develop an intuitive understanding of governmental processes by being "close to political forces." "Close" need not imply personal political interaction, but it does imply an empathy for what motivates various political actors both personally and substantively.

One simple way to cultivate an awareness of political legitimacy is to first approach all public policy issues by assuming that government knows what it is doing. For those individuals with the common American cynicism about government, this can be difficult, but the approach will typically reveal a lot about the politics of business/government relations. For example, some rules and procedures seem to accomplish nothing. A rationalist might conclude that this reflects bureaucratic incompetence. While such might be the case, it might be more revealing to first assume that this result is intentional—after all, doctors have long recognized that the appropriate prescription for some patients is nothing but a placebo. Politicians may well be as adept as practiced doctors in dealing in placebos.

In the area of regional economic policy, for example, many economists have been critical of the Economic Development Administration (EDA) within the Department of Commerce for its programs of aid to depressed regions. These programs are frequently criticized for having rather limited impact on regional depression and, thus, economists have argued against them on grounds of economic inefficiency. A more political and less economic view might acknowledge that the government can do little to turn depressed communities around with any reasonable allocation of economic resources and legal coercion. A government can, nonetheless, signal its compassion for the plight of the troubled people with programs of aid. In so doing it might even succeed in smoothing a period of difficult adjustment.

Sometimes government is viewed as redundant, merely duplicating what market institutions already do well. Again, this may represent political meddling and incompetence, or it may reflect the critical role that government plays in giving legitimacy to market outcomes. For example, when energy prices were rising rapidly in the 1970s, many economists counseled against a formal government program of price controls; others contended that economists were unwise in advising against *any* governmental role in the price-setting process. Some of us might have found it quite silly and unnecessarily expensive to post stickers on gasoline pumps indicating the legal maximum price for gasoline, but to many citizens confused, less well informed, and suspicious of an industrial conspiracy, such posting might well have been comforting and thus may have conferred legitimacy to the subsequent market determination of prices.

Yet what might have been comforting to consumers might not have been equally comforting to business interests. Indeed, during this same period many people in the business community felt that government was unduly antagonistic to the energy industry. Rather than view government involvement in energy prices as inept meddling, it is worth considering the political merits of the adversarial posture the government assumed. It is not hard to imagine some of the serious political repercussions if the national government had appeared to side with oil interests and failed to regulate or post prices during this difficult time.

This discussion is not intended to argue in favor of government's position on these matters but to suggest that an initial presumption that government *did* know what it was doing might yield insights into political processes. Such insights, it is worth noting, can be gained even if subsequent analysis reveals that government policy was, in fact, misguided.

As soon as one begins to pay attention to political legitimacy, it becomes clear that many of the advantages of the marketplace stem from political acceptance of the prices set in these markets as "fair." This fairness results in part from the political legitimacy of market transactions in a capitalistic society as well as from the economic efficiency of such transactions. Government, through its system of rules and constraints on business, plays an important role in maintaining—and sometimes undermining —the political legitimacy of markets.

An appreciation of the importance of political legitimacy to a sustainable energy business created a curious positioning of policy advocates in 1982. Many students of past energy crises had recognized that an unregulated market would be the best public policy for handling a future oil supply disruption. The Reagan Administration advocated this view. Interestingly, however, the Reagan policy advisors also advocated a complete hands-off government position during an energy emergency— even to the point of opposing stand-by authority for presidential intervention. By contrast, an industry trade group called the National Petroleum Council (NPC) sought a specific federal contingency plan for handling another oil supply disruption, should it occur.[1] Neither the NPC nor the Reagan Administration disagreed on the merits of decontrolled prices, but they differed on what was necessary to allow market-set prices to be politically acceptable. The NPC saw the advantage of an explicit governmental policy to provide credibility to the otherwise unrestrained operation of the market. The Reagan advisors felt that the mere existence of such authority itself undermined the legitimacy of market transactions. It is worth observing that agreement on the political nature of the problem did not lead to agreement on the preferred solution. Nor, for that matter, is it at all clear which position reflects greater political sensitivity and sophistication. In politics, both means and ends are highly judgmental.

The need for attention to issues of political legitimacy is not reserved for national crises. Most chemical companies today recognize that the public's concern about toxic chemicals in the environment is a legitimate public issue, although the situation is not yet, at least, a national crisis of the magnitude of the nation's past energy problems. The companies may disagree on the severity of the problem. They may disagree on the source of responsibility. They may also disagree on the solution. But they do not dismiss the issue merely because it has not reached the crisis stage. Instead, many firms have actively embraced the problem, taking action well beyond the requirements of current law or economics. They have funded research, the results of which may not always appear favorable to their interests. And they are very active at virtually all levels of government.

All of this attention reflects an appreciation of the fact that legislation often follows public sentiment. It is the political legitimacy of the hazardous waste issue and the attendant economic risks that justify top management's attention to it, not merely the existence of some complex law with arcane regulatory provisions.

LEARN HOW THE LEGISLATIVE PROCESS WORKS

The second rule to follow in pursuit of better understanding of regulatory issues is to learn how the legislative process *really* works. One view of legislation is that it is merely a formal codification of the fact that an issue is politically legitimate. Much of the important political work takes place prior to legislation in building and forming consensus. Managers who understand this learn how the legislative process works before the relevant piece of legislation concerns them. This, of course, implies more political homework; it also implies a frequent enough presence in Washington and state capitals to cultivate an understanding of processes that bear little resemblance to those described in high school civics texts.

Because so much of the legislative process does involve the formal codification that an issue is politically legitimate, sophisticated actors appreciate that the "no legislation" alternative is often not practical on any major issue. But if legislation is itself evidence that an issue is politically legitimate, it does not always follow that the content of that legislation is central to this primary political objective. Accordingly, it becomes important for business managers to understand how to deal with legislative details. While it may sometimes appear that the most sophisticated private sector actors take legislation as given and then "wheel and deal" on its administration, this is not the case. Many successful intervenors in regulatory processes do achieve their success in program administration, but it is also true that they often try to get into legislation the little "hooks" they can grab onto subsequently in the administration process. This kind of sophisticated action, however, is hardly for the uninitiated. It typically requires experience and prior active involvement in the legislative process.

PAY CLOSE ATTENTION TO THE PROCESS OF POLICY ADMINISTRATION

The third rule is to pay close attention to the process of policy administration. In the final analysis, no matter how detailed and specific a piece of legislation, the implementing agency typically possesses sufficient administrative discretion to accommodate a wide range of policy outcomes—and thus economic outcomes. Airline deregulation is the classic illustration. While it is true that Congress ultimately passed a bill to deregulate that industry, a good deal of what the new law allowed had been done administratively by Civil Aeronautics Board (CAB) chairmen John Robson and Alfred Kahn before legislation passed—despite the fact that for thirty years people had argued that the CAB could not deregulate the industry because it was constrained by law.[2] Robson and Kahn did not feel so constrained. They were able to make a deregulation policy stand because they understood *both* the underlying political legitimacy behind the deregulation movement and how to use administrative discretion within the regulatory process.

SYSTEMATICALLY EXAMINE THE COMPETITIVE IMPLICATIONS OF GOVERNMENT ACTION

Good competitors who understand how government operates can be expected to systematically examine the competitive implications of government action. Cummins Engine, for example, has a separate corporate staff assigned the role of preparing competitive analyses of proposed government regulatory and legislative actions. This staff asks what a regulatory initiative means to the company and whether the initiative represents sound public policy—not merely to second-guess government analysts, but to help understand the underlying legitimacy of the proposed regulatory intervention. The staff does not restrict its analyses to policies that affect only Cummins but addresses issues relevant to its customers, host communities, and employees as well.[3]

With this sophisticated analytical capability, Cummins Engine has developed a highly regarded reputation for being a socially responsible company that deals in an honest and forthright manner on a wide range of public policy issues.

It is worth stressing that there need be no conflict between exploiting regulation for competitive gain and doing so in a socially responsible manner. If it is true that all regulations create winners and losers, then this is true of good regulations as well as bad regulations. Sophisticated analysis of both competitive opportunities and social responsibilities allows a strategy exploiting what is otherwise judged to be socially responsible regulation. Such a strategy has the further virtue that good legislation is more likely to survive in the long run than bad legislation, which, by definition, contains the seeds of its own destruction.

An example illustrates the sophistication of the Cummins strategy: air emissions controls for heavy-duty trucks. Officials at Cummins realized that scientific information was going to play a very important role in deciding what those regulations would be. Cummins' interests in these regulations did not necessarily coincide with those of its competition, as the Iron Law would suggest. Some of these competitors had far bigger research budgets than Cummins.

What could Cummins do? It helped create something called the Health Effects Institute. Today the EPA and the truck-manufacturing companies funnel money for research on heavy-duty truck emissions into this private organization. All parties have agreed in advance that they would not "compete" on the basis of information but rather would employ this institute as a somewhat more neutral and objective source of technical input. By the way, that organization is run by a former Cummins employee.

LOOK FOR WAYS TO USE GOVERNMENT REGULATION AS A COMPETITIVE WEAPON

The fifth and final rule to improve understanding of regulatory processes is to actively seek ways to use regulations as a competitive weapon. For example, air emissions controls for automobiles require the use of catalytic converters. The essence of a catalytic converter is a ceramic substrate manufactured by Corning through which the exhaust gases must pass. Recently Corning adapted this technology for use in residential wood-burning stoves. This development was coupled with public testimony before regulatory authorities on the increasingly serious pollution problems created by wood burning in high-density suburban neighborhoods.[4] It is important to stress that if such testimony led to regulations, the rules would not only be to Corning's competitive advantage but would address a real environmental problem that could use a solution. And if not adopted, the experience in the political process would itself be valuable to Corning, if only to signal to regulators the company's creativity in addressing environmental issues.

A similar situation involved the chain-saw safety issue described in chapter 3.[5] One of the toughest questions of safety regulation in the chain-saw industry has to do with saw kickback—the risk of serious personal injury when a saw kicks back from the item being cut. One competitor invented an anti-kickback device for its saws, while another invented a chain saw less likely to kick back. Not surprisingly, each firm wanted a regulatory standard consistent with its technology. As of this writing, the issue is not resolved, but there is hope that as the two firms jockey for competitive advantage, the key public policy issues surrounding this debate will be thoroughly aired, facilitating achievement of legitimate policy goals.

Influence the Process

Understanding political and regulatory processes is necessary for an effective strategy for dealing with government, but it is not always sufficient. Often it is also necessary to influence the process directly. There are at least four rules for successful intervention:

1. Be actively present.
2. Take preemptive action.
3. Take individual action.
4. Use information as a weapon.

BE ACTIVELY PRESENT

An active presence in governmental affairs is often essential to successful intervention. Such presence need not—and perhaps should not—be restricted to issues of obvious corporate relevance. Because politicians deal in communication, the more often they hear from someone, the easier it may be for them to gauge both credibility and political orientation.

The Cummins Engine office that looks at the competitive effects of various public policies systematically does sophisticated economic analysis of the consequences for society of the most important pieces of legislation. It shares those analyses with the key political actors. This serves several purposes. For one thing, it lets people know that Cummins Engine does good, honest, objective analysis. This builds credibility. But just as important, it keeps Cummins out front and visible whenever a reputation for good work is critical to the firm's interests.

TAKE PREEMPTIVE ACTION

Successful intervention into the process of government often depends on thoughtful preemptive action. Once rules and regulations are in place, winners and losers have been created, and the winners, in particular, can become entrenched. Moreover, rules are established as part of the ritual of political accommodation and compromise. The introduction of a new party to these deliberations after decisions have already been made can complicate the task facing politicians who may be sensitive to a particular plaintiff.

It would be an overstatement to say that preemptive action is always preferred to reaction, because successful intervention can occur in a reactive mode. Previous chapters have described such cases, including the experience of George Lockwood and the Monterey Abalone Farms. Yet Lockwood's experience in this regard is itself revealing, for while he was reasonably successful with a reactive posture, he too soon discovered the merits of preemptive action.

Ultimately, the appeal of preemptive action stems from the very nature of political and regulatory processes. Because government tries to be responsive to micro-level impacts, the process can only bog down when confronted with a series of sequential interventions. It is simply easier to accommodate competing interests when all competing interests are known.

Moreover, preemptive action implies, almost by definition, an ongoing involvement in the political process, with the implications for both understanding and credibility such a posture implies.

And finally, preemptive action releases politicians from accusations of capitulating to special interests, as subsequent accommodations in policy might be interpreted to be.

TAKE INDIVIDUAL ACTION

The Iron Law of Public Policy reveals that all policy interventions will create winners and losers within the regulated sector. This reality places limits on what can be accomplished through joint action. Indeed, because there are winners and losers, coordinated business responses to government policy can create a bias in the process of weighing special interests.

According to the political theory, various special interests bring their individual cases before, say, the Congress. As the Congress evaluates the merits of various claims, a compromise is reached that presumably serves the interests of society at large despite the fact that society at large is represented solely by its elected officials and these special interest groups. Thus environmental interest groups presumably represent society's interests in environmental matters, while business represents society's interests in economic matters. In the ideal world, the compromise of these interests would yield the socially preferred public policy.

But the dynamics of special interest politics are often quite different from the simple theory. Suppose two environmental groups decide to combine their political forces. If one group prefers a tough position and the other a more moderate one, it may well be possible that both can agree not on a central position but rather on one toward the side of stringency. Call it left of center, if you will. Why? Because even the moderate group will be satisfied if the resulting rules prove tougher than they would have otherwise chosen since a tougher policy only means more of the environmental protection both groups seek.

Now consider the allegedly countervailing business interests. If they combine their political forces, can they agree on a position that is right of center and thus offset the opposition's pro-regulation bias? Not necessarily. Unlike the environmentalists, who may be able to agree on the desirability of a tougher policy, not all economic interests, because of the operation of the Iron Law of Public Policy, would prefer a lenient policy. Thus, business interests may tend closer to a centrist position from the start.

The resulting political compromise of a more centrist economic position and a left-of-center environmentalist position could easily be a policy tilted more to environmental interests than the body politic might prefer.

Consider the case of auto emissions controls. The economic trade-offs in this policy area are substantial. Presumably, the environmentalists were looking out for one side of these trade-offs and the business interests the other. Yet experience suggests that the resulting compromise in policy was tilted more to the environmentalist side than may have been in the public interest. One possible reason for this is that while business interests were to some degree consonant with consumers' economic interests, there were clear divergences in the interests of individual automakers and the consumers they served. Thus, for example, General Motors had a vested interest in catalytic converter technology, which required a relatively stringent standard—and presumably a willingness to compromise in favor of policies more stringent than consumer advocacy alone might imply.

This is not to "blame" GM for stringent pollution control laws. Rather it is to observe that the competitive interests of individual firms necessarily differ due to the operation of the

Iron Law. This can lead to group positions on policy matters that shift decisions away from those that might occur in the absence of coordinated business action.

Sometimes, of course, an individual competitor's interests are best served by attaining the outcome supported by joint action, but for this position to be viable, some of the participants in the joint response must not be well informed of their own interests or must have some overriding interest in joint action—perhaps because of some other policy issue facing the firm. In any case, over time, as firms become more sophisticated in their governmental dealings, one might expect to see more individual action.

Trends in this direction are already evident in the proliferation of trade associations organized around some very narrow political interests. For example, different trade groups represent natural gas producers who dig deep wells and those who dig shallow ones. This same trend is evident in the relative decline in political clout of some of the largest trade associations, which have their own internal problems of establishing political consensus.

This phenomenon, of course, is not limited to issues involving business and government but is the logical outgrowth of the increasing political sophistication of individual special interests. Thus, over time, the nation's major political parties have found the task facing them greater and greater as smaller groups representing narrow but more homogeneous interests have thrived.

USE INFORMATION AS A WEAPON

The last rule for successful intervention in regulatory processes is perhaps the most important: use information as an aggressive political weapon. Most regulatory processes are information-driven, and control of this information can be critical to success in the regulatory process. When William Ruckelshaus left the Environmental Protection Agency after his first stint as administrator, he went to the Weyerhaeuser Company. Shortly after taking this new position he was interviewed by the editors of *Fortune* magazine and asked what strategy he would implement to deal with Washington.[6] His response was simple: "Our strategy will be to capture the data." Ruckelshaus went on to describe the importance of controlling information. By "control" he did not imply either giving wrong information or withholding information. Rather, he noted, being aware of the facts—whatever they might imply for the corporation—was better than being surprised by someone else's facts, even if the other facts were correct.

In the process of political economy, business has an inherent comparative advantage in most economic and much scientific data. A strategy of "capturing the data" is merely recognition and exploitation of this reality. Moreover, since the Iron Law means that someone wins and someone loses no matter what, a corporate position based on objective information is clearly preferred both socially and economically to one predicated on faulty information.

Information is also the avenue to decision makers in a bottom-up regulatory organization. Career bureaucrats can often attribute their power to the importance of data and the need for a sound factual basis to public policy making. An information-based strategy exploits this.

The use of information as a competitive weapon in political affairs need not be restricted to data themselves. It can include control of the methodologies that will be used to analyze the existing data. For example, in arguing against some of the more stringent provisions of the Clean Water Act, the American Paper Institute (API) introduced studies that showed the economic consequences of compelling firms to divert scarce capital resources from plant modernization and expansion to pollution control.[7] The API study had several key attributes.

First, it addressed empirically an issue that had *both* intuitive political appeal and economic merit. Other business interests had made a similar claim but had failed to substantiate it. The API study thus touched a political nerve while at the same time it highlighted a legitimate economic concern that professional analysts could not ignore—and, indeed, did not want to ignore because of the professional challenge of dealing with such an issue.

The API study had the further merit that it placed the industry in a "no lose" situation. If the report proved persuasive, environmental rules might be relaxed; but if it did not persuade policy makers, it at least had the merit of highlighting in the minds of technocrats the important issues of regulatory timing and capital formation that ultimately could not be avoided. And if the research spawned by the study proved that the issue of capital diversion was less important than the API had thought, then any subsequent political loss on the point would also be less important.

This last point is often lost in the give-and-take of regulatory affairs: to "lose" a regulatory battle on the merits of the case is clearly preferable to losing it due to ignorance. Ultimately, it is this point that argues most strongly for a regulatory strategy based on information.

Be a Winner

There is no reason to believe that an effective corporate strategy for dealing with government should be different from any other corporate strategy. Corporate strategies typically have got to be put on paper. They have to be articulated in the daily affairs of the corporation; they have to be studied; and they have to reflect a sense of shared values within the organization. Corporate strategy for dealing with government must meet this same set of standards.

Thus a good corporate regulatory strategy will likely involve a formal program to identify opportunities to use policy and regulatory instruments for competitive gain. To ensure that this is done in a socially responsible way—and the Iron Law tells us that there is no reason not to be socially responsible when pursuing competitive advantages by regulatory means—this activity should presumably be coordinated with the firm's program for social responsibility.

It is central to recognize that a corporate strategy for exploiting the business opportunities created by regulation and government action differs in a fundamental way from programs of social responsibility, even though the two might be linked. The primary objective of a program of social responsibility is to ensure that the firm is a good corporate citizen; the objective of a formal strategy for dealing with government is improved corporate competitiveness and profitability.

Because all public policy and regulatory issues involve personal and political value judgments, it is important to organize the *internal* corporate political process for establishing company positions on social matters. As in government, this consensus-building process should be based on a strong analytical capacity. Again, as in government, it is also advisable to have formal organizational procedures for mediating internal political disputes. In this regard, it seems unwise to resort to ad hoc procedures when sensitive issues materialize because it is under precisely these conditions that the merits of a formal system with which people are experienced will prove most useful. Ad hoc or unfamiliar procedures almost always strike some individuals as arbitrary, thus compounding management's political challenge.

And, of course, this internal process needs to be integrated with the formal mechanisms for dealing with *external* political processes. This formal process, as the preceding discussion has suggested, should be based on the development of a prelegislative presence, credibility, and understanding. It should include an understanding of the legislative process itself as well as various administrative contacts. Because the government can be a bottom-up organization, these administrative contacts should not be restricted to top corporate officials, but should occur at all levels of both the corporation and the government.

One advantage of this approach is that it can simultaneously exploit the substantial political expertise of the existing corporate managerial structure. It is worth pointing out that while many companies hire government specialists, often the members of the management team most proficient at political affairs are plant managers who, by virtue of daily grass-roots political contact, have many untapped political skills.

And, of course, this external political process should not be restricted to trade group actions but should include the capacity for individual corporate action.

Now, it might appear that this description of a formal corporate strategy for dealing with governmental and regulatory affairs applies only to large corporations and represents a substantial increase in fixed costs. Neither needs to be the case. The existence of a formal procedure need not imply a large fixed staff; many of the best political specialists within the firm—for example, plant managers—are already on board and sensitive to political issues.

More important, a corporate strategy for dealing with governmental and regulatory affairs should not be viewed as "another costly overhead expense." Rather it should be considered a basic and fundamental activity of good business management. The goal of such a strategy is not merely social responsibility —although that is hardly an undesirable objective; it is enhanced profitability and improved competitive position. Ultimately, a corporation's true contributions to society are measured in these two dimensions, for, after all, corporations were created by acts of government in the first place to pursue these objectives.

Chapter 11

A Public Manager's

Perspective

Most people recognize that managers in the private sector must integrate political and regulatory realities into the formulation of strategy and day-to-day management decision making. Indeed, it is taken as given—often begrudgingly—that good managers in the private sector must have skills in political economy as well as business. Far fewer people recognize that public policy makers, to be effective, have a similar need to cultivate skills in political economy. They must factor private-sector competitive and political responses into their policy development and implementation processes. Unfortunately, in the minds of many, public policy makers who are politically sophisticated are often viewed as opportunistic "wheeler-dealers" operating on the fringe of ethical behavior. This asymmetrical view of how managers on each side of the business/government interface should act in response to the decisions of the other has important implications for the competitive effects of government actions and, at present, limits the effectiveness of public policy.

This chapter explores the various motivations and operating strategies public managers can use to address issues related to the competitive impact of government policy. It attempts to demonstrate that good public policy, just like good private management, necessitates an understanding of competition when government matters.

The Private versus the Public Manager

To appreciate the public manager's perspective on policies affecting business, it is worthwhile to contrast the images of public- and private-sector managers. Consider first managers in the private sector. They are typically viewed as pragmatic, competent, and legitimately motivated by self-interest. Pragmatism necessitates dealing directly and aggressively with government issues even if the ideal world would be free of political intervention. Competence suggests that the managers will work in a sophisticated "strategic" manner. They will not view dealings with government as exercises in high school civics but as a serious game of politics with significant financial implications. And self-interest requires the pursuit of those public policies that contribute most to the profitability of the enterprise and opposition to policies that do not serve its interest.

Contrast the image of managers in the public sector. They are often viewed as idealistic, analytical, and apolitical "public servants." Idealism necessitates dealing with business/government issues in the abstract by identifying "optimal" policies based on fundamental principles of political science and economics. Analysis implies that public-sector decision makers will deal strictly with the technical aspects of the business/government relationship. The public manager is often viewed as pursuing goals in the "optimal" way as though government authority alone was sufficient to get the job done. And finally, since all government policies create winners and losers, the public decision makers must avoid both the appearance and substance of responding to these political realities and maintain an apolitical stance.

The Elusive Pursuit of the Optimal Policy

While this particular characterization of the public decision maker is a bit overdrawn, it is useful nonetheless for it sheds light on one major type of public policy response to business/government issues: the pursuit of the apolitical "optimal policy." Consider the massive economics literature that argues for using the price mechanism as the optimal solution to many public policy problems. This policy recommendation manifests itself in areas as diverse as effluent fees for pollution control to the auctioning off of rights to import shoes and steel. Analysts often examine such policies, aimed as they are at achieving goals of economic efficiency, as strictly economic matters, with little formal or sophisticated treatment of their political or managerial ramifications. Indeed, focusing formal analysis on political issues is considered by many public-sector analysts as a contradiction in terms: analysis deals in objective considerations, while politics is purely subjective.

Despite the enthusiasm among economists for the use of price incentives to solve policy problems, more politically sensitive practitioners often tend to be skeptical of efficiency-oriented pricing schemes for both administrative and political reasons. They recognize that prices give desirable incentives, but they also recognize that prices are difficult to set—especially for activities subject to government regulation. (If they were easy to set, the goods or service might well be provided by the private sector in the first place!) Moreover, one person's price is another person's revenue. If problems of administrative feasibility are overcome, arguments over the distribution of revenues will often block the use of price mechanisms. These practical difficulties notwithstanding, analysts often choose the use of prices as the optimal policy particularly when it comes to regulating business.

There is a frequently used expression that "the perfect is the enemy of the good," implying, of course, that the elusive search for the optimal value-free solution to any public policy problem can have the negative effect of deferring the implementation of less-than-perfect but otherwise quite acceptable policy alternatives. Effective managers in the public sector, perhaps more than anywhere else, are aware of this truism. Yet a major consequence of the public's image of the government manager as an apolitical public administrator is that it forces the conversation —if not the reality—of the policy debate to examine optimal solutions to business/government problems.

This response is, of course, naïve. For one thing, it presumes the ability to identify an optimal policy. Such is often not the case because of the highly complex and multidimensional goals of government.

Take, for example, a recent recommendation of economists from the Federal Trade Commission to auction off the rights to import steel into the United States. Such a policy was seen as a means of protecting U.S. workers and companies from the adverse effects of import competition without giving foreign suppliers the benefits of higher prices at the same time. (Presumably, the bids would capture all the benefits of higher steel prices created by import restraint that would otherwise accrue to foreign producers.) The recommendation had intuitive appeal. While the FTC economists were opposed to any form of import restraint, they felt that at least a quota that was auctioned off would have two desirable attributes. First, only those countries and firms willing to pay for the right to sell steel in the United States would be able to do so. And second, the federal treasury would benefit from the auction revenues. This would reduce, although not eliminate, the net social cost to the U.S. economy of an otherwise undesirable trade restraint policy because the benefit of the higher prices induced by trade restraint would not accrue to foreign producers.

Given these two desirable attributes, a policy of auctioning import quotas looks attractive. But there are other considerations. For example, trade restraint is supposed to be a temporary policy aimed at protecting industry only until it undergoes revitalization. What if political actors, seeing the deficit-ridden federal government, like the idea of a new revenue source? We all know how "temporary" the telephone excise taxes of World War II have been. Moreover, those countries willing to pay for quota rights might be willing to do so precisely because they are desperate for the dollars U.S. sales represent. In the complex world of international finance, the need to use scarce dollars to buy quota rights could mean default on loans from U.S. banks. Thus the federal revenues generated by such an auction might be needed to bail out the international banking system and do little to ameliorate the federal government's financial problems.

The point of this example, of course, is not to argue for or against the sale of import quota rights. Nor is it to dismiss the pursuit of "optimal" policies as unavoidably naïve; rather it is to observe that what is considered "optimal" is far from obvious in a world of complicated economic interactions and policy trade-offs. In such a world, the sophisticated policy maker should not become preoccupied with the identification and implementation of the optimal policy but rather focus efforts on the pursuit of a policy strategy that, over time, can be expected to evolve in that direction. Yet, in pursuing such a strategy, the public manager is nonetheless compelled to carry on the debate *as if* the issue were the implementation here and now of the optimal policy. This discrepancy between the language and the substance of the public debate over business/government issues makes the public policy maker vulnerable to certain avenues of political attack from advocates and opponents of government intervention.

Continuing with our trade policy example, it is generally well recognized—and has been for well over a hundred years— though some would disagree, that the optimal long-run trade policy is free trade. To the sophisticated policy maker, the test of the optimality of auctioning import quota rights is not its attractiveness near term but its implications for the free-trade goal. While the more naïve policy maker may pursue the short-term optimal solution that such a pricing scheme might imply, the sophisticated policy maker keeps a strategic eye on the long-term objections and asks what a "successful" auction might mean for the likelihood that an undesirable policy of "temporary" trade restraint will be perpetuated. In the world of "objective" and dispassionate analysis, however, the quantifiable estimates of the benefits of auctioned quotas are compared to the costs of having no such auction process. The analyst, unlike the policy manager, does not view the decision as one play in a complicated political game but as a straightforward static comparison of two alternatives. The consequence of engaging the debate in a language different from the substance of the underlying political decisions is that there is a tendency toward incremental versus strategic decision making by public managers in business/government affairs.

This tendency is further reinforced in another way. In the public's view, government decision makers are not always to be trusted to manage a sophisticated business/government relationship. Consequently, public managers are placed under such stringent standards of accountability that the successful execution of their assignments is often jeopardized. This is especially true when strategic management considerations encourage public managers to take actions that, on the surface, are contrary to what an "objective analysis" might indicate.

Accountability to Process Not Outcome

While it is difficult to object to such extensive management accountability in concept, it is easy to object to it in practice. All too often this preoccupation with public manager accountability in business/government matters is not only ineffective but dysfunctional. One reason for this is that public managers tend to be held accountable almost exclusively to process and rarely to outcome.

Two examples illustrate the distinction. Shortly after the oil market disruption of 1979, the vice-president of operations for a Fortune 100 firm faced an inquiry from the Department of

Energy (DOE), which was, at that time, aggressively searching for ways the nation could use less oil. To further this objective, the DOE required this manufacturing firm to identify ways in which it could convert existing oil-fired industrial boilers to coal. Actual conversion was not required, but an inventory of potential conversions was deemed useful to energy policy makers.

The first inquiry went directly to the operating vice-president. The request was taken seriously. The corporation's resources were immediately directed to compiling the requested information. The effort was apparently thorough and expeditious. Indeed, virtually all individuals involved—particularly the operating vice-president himself—saw their efforts as part of a patriotic duty during what was recognized as a time of national need.

Rather than exploit this patriotic motivation, as would be the inclination of any otherwise unconstrained manager, DOE officials were forced to meet procedural tests for accountability. Consequently, despite the seriousness with which this individual and his staff had undertaken this assignment, their report was immediately returned to the firm's headquarters for lack of a signature from a corporate officer above the level of the operating vice-president. While the legalisms of such a signature are understandable, the immediate impact on the data collection team was debilitating: they had been loyal to their country, but their country had not trusted their commitment.

To compound matters, as part of DOE's "accountability" procedures, this same report was later singled out for audit. Thus the newly signed report was sent back once again for verification of its accuracy. The consequence of this entire effort was an extremely unhappy senior corporate executive whose response was (to paraphrase) "First they said I needed my boss's signature and then they called me a liar. I'll be damned if I will ever cooperate with them again except as the letter of the law requires."[1]

Had the public manager been accountable for outcome—good data, collected at reasonable cost—rather than for procedure—signatures and audits—this adverse development might have been avoided. There is no telling how many other seemingly inconsequential events such as this have occurred, creating distrust, animosity, and the attendant costs of an unnecessarily combative business/government relationship.

While the need for formal procedures and accountable public officials is obvious, the manner in which formality and accountability are exercised is central to the effectiveness of the public manager's dealings with business firms. "Going by the book"[2] is not so much the problem as the naïve public view that the book itself must be highly detailed and must prohibit public managers from exercising discretion.

Process accountability often manifests itself in ways even more tangibly damaging to both the public good and the interests of responsible executives than the DOE case just cited, as a second example illustrates. In chapter 9 we noted that a state regulator in Massachusetts, charged with recommending approval or disapproval of pesticides for use within the state, recommended the banning of a potentially dangerous chemical that had very limited applications but was extremely valuable when needed. The official's reasoning was as follows: she was accountable to a set of rules regarding the licensing of pesticides. The procedural consequences of licensing a chemical that later proved harmful were great. On the other hand, the subsequent finding that an unlicensed chemical had been misused—and caused harm—would merely vindicate her recommendation to ban it in the first place. While she acknowledged that actual use of the chemical would not likely drop with its ban, since it was readily available and no alternative existed, that was "an enforcement problem" and outside her jurisdiction. She also conceded that law-abiding exterminators would not use the chemical and use would thus be confined to unscrupulous operators. This admittedly would give a competitive advantage to the dishonest firms and might even increase the likelihood of misuse.

Because the official was held accountable to *process* and not to *outcome,* it was logical for her to pursue the action she did.

Indeed, when questioned about the merits of her decision, she innocently acknowledged that her job was to license chemicals —a process—not to ensure their proper use—an outcome.

This preoccupation with process accountability rather than a responsibility for policy outcome is a major characteristic of regulatory activity. One of the greatest public policy challenges is to allow so-called nonpolitical public decision makers—commissioners, civil servants, and the like—the discretion they need to manage outcomes without losing the accountability to process demanded by our political system. This preoccupation stems largely from a conception of the ideal public manager as strictly apolitical—someone who just does the job without giving in to political pressure, without showing favoritism, and without personal value judgments—in contrast to the real-world public manager, who, unless made to go scrupuously by the book, will succumb to political pressure. This idealistic apoliticism is perhaps the most naïve of all public characterizations of the public decision maker's task, yet it is an important reality with which the public manager—and, of course, indirectly, the private manager—must deal. The view is naïve because in a world in which *all* policy actions create winners and losers, there are, by definition, political ramifications to all government decisions affecting business. Unfortunately, civil servants are often compelled to pretend to ignore these political realities or address them in the guise of applying formal procedures. While sophisticated policy makers recognize the inevitability of this political dimension to their activities and pragmatically and unapologetically manage regulatory affairs with these political realities in mind, procedural accountability all too often compels good public managers to ignore true public values because of the need to meet accountability criteria.

Managing the Iron Law

Sophisticated public management of the business/government interface begins with an appreciation of the Iron Law: there are always winners and losers. Rather than ignore or merely attempt to minimize these gains and losses, sophisticated decision makers manage them in ways that advance the strategic interests of their organization. Thus we saw in chapter 3, when discussing the ways in which regulatory compliance costs for water pollution control differed among competitors, that regulators apparently managed the creation of both winners and losers to help reduce industrial opposition to stringent pollution control requirements. They did this by developing what policy analysts might consider an uneconomic policy. Nothing in the technical analysis of water pollution control policy supported their approach; to the contrary, such analysis identified the inconsistencies. In the more complicated world of regulatory policies, there were no such inconsistencies.

On the one hand, conscious management of gains and losses is potentially quite dangerous, given the obvious possibilities for corruption and abuse. On the other hand, efforts to foreclose such management are bound to fail—the Iron Law cannot be repealed. Thus excessive restraint on the activities of government officials through increasingly detailed accountability to process offers little prospect for successfully creating the most desirable policy outcomes. It does run the risk, however, of creating a bureaucratic environment in which the winners and losers are confronted with such arcane and detailed institutional procedures that the real political consequences are effectively invisible to the very public whose interests these extreme requirements for accountability are presumed to protect.

Corruption is not the only danger. Sophisticated public regulators can often use their authority to create winners and losers to entrench their own interests. In this context, both winners and losers become "assets" to be managed. Winners, of course, are assets, because as beneficiaries of public policy actions they are presumably a source of political support. Losers also become assets, however, since their existence and political strength can be used to marshal public resources to the agency or function in question as well. For example, a regulatory program that causes harm to small businesses might create political pressure for a budgetary authorization to the agency administering the program to fund a new effort to deal with the small-business "problem."

There are some sad ironies to this process. The first is that the value of losers to the public manager stems primarily from dependence. Consequently, maintenance of dependence can become an important bureaucratic goal. Industries and firms that seek public support in times of crisis often ignore this reality. The ailing steel industry, for example, has enthusiastically sought public protection for the last two decades, whether in the form of import restraint, less stringent pollution controls, or implicit subsidies through capital depreciation schedules. The political strength of the Congressional Steel Caucus is typically viewed as a benefit to this industry—but it is a benefit only so long as the industry is in distress and needs the help the caucus can promise. A highly profitable domestic steel industry would not need this special political support and would thus reduce the political leverage of groups like the Steel Caucus.

Stated differently, the political process has a clear incentive not to let the U.S. steel industry sink in its current sea of troubles. It similarly has little incentive to see it swim independently to a safe harbor. Rather there are strong political incentives to keep the industry's nose just above water so it neither sinks nor swims but remains dependent on the actions of public policy makers.

There is no better evidence of this political tendency to impose control as a price for favorable public action than in a recent decision of the International Trade Commission (ITC). Bethlehem Steel, severely affected by the loss of market share to foreign suppliers, petitioned the ITC for relief from import competition. In its decision to recommend such relief, the commission also advocated the pursuit of an active industrial policy to "assist" the industry in its restructuring. While Bethlehem's management was clearly interested in the benefits of import restraint, to its stockholders and employees, it was far less enthusiastic about the quid pro quo of an aggressive federal industrial policy. Yet such a demand was perfectly predictable. Indeed, one of Bethlehem's own witnesses before the commission, Felix Rohatyn, had called for such a federal policy when testifying on the company's behalf.[3]

To maintain the political control that comes from the ability to create winners and losers, sophisticated public managers recognize the importance of regulatory change. After all, once a rule is in place, winners and losers are established. In the regulatory environment, change—or the threat of change—offers the only political advantage because change is the source of gains and losses.

This principle is well recognized in the discussion of public taxation, where there is a common expression that "there is no tax like an old tax." The notion is that all taxes have their own inefficiencies and inequities and create their own winners and losers, but if left in place long enough, individuals and firms will be able to modify their behavior to accommodate most of these idiosyncracies.

The same notion applies to regulation and other government policies: if left in place long enough, consumers and investors can usually accommodate, albeit with varying degrees of success.

While stability may be a virtue of good policy, it is not necessarily a virtue of good politics or good management of business/government issues, since instability creates the power to create the gains and losses so critical to bureaucratic management of the business/government process. The sophisticated public manager is sensitive to the creation of winners and losers, because the associated power is politically valuable.

Managing the Data—A Public Manager's View

The sophisticated public manager is also sensitive to the ways in which private actors can themselves influence this process. Chapter 10 noted that one of the most effective devices available to private actors for influencing policy was "control of the data." By controlling the information base and the methodologies by which these data are analyzed, private actors can exercise a good deal of influence in the business/government process. Sophisticated public managers recognize this reality and take steps to avoid "methodological capture" of agency decision making not only by business interests but by other managers within the government.

Actually, methodological capture is itself an "advance play" in the increasingly sophisticated game of business/government relations. Typically, at the onset of a regulatory intervention, private interests control the data but public interests control the budget—and thus the method—for analyzing the data. For a variety of reasons, access to the data cannot be denied to public authorities for very long. For one thing, they typically possess or can acquire subpoena power. More important, as data are made available to public authorities, private interests, playing to a perceived strength, tend to escalate the data requirements. This is a temporary victory at best, since regulators eventually catch up with more sophisticated requests. Ultimately, the issue becomes not the data but the methodology used to analyze it.

A classic but far from unique case of the data escalation problem entailed an EPA study of the economic impact of pollution controls on the paper industry. To undertake this study, the EPA hired an independent contractor. This contractor recommended the use of so-called hypothetical plant data—information provided by engineering firms for fictitious plants designed on the drawing board to represent actual plants in the field. The proposal had the merits of providing consistent data quickly and inexpensively; it had the disadvantage of not providing "real" data.

To solve this alleged problem, industry interests proposed the use of actual plant data. To acquire this information would necessitate a costly survey and thus put pressure on the EPA's limited research budget. Under then-current paperwork rules, federally funded surveys were strictly controlled by the Office of Management and Budget (OMB). To minimize red tape, the contractor proposed asking nine questions of nine firms and designed the questions so that they could all be answered by reference to information already filed publicly with the Securities and Exchange Commission. The EPA would bear the added direct but nominal expense.

The industry group responded that the survey idea was fine, but the choice of nine interviewees would necessarily be arbitrary and, therefore, unacceptable. The EPA reluctantly agreed to survey the managements of more than six-hundred plants in the industry and to seek OMB approval to do so.

Data escalation did not stop there. Rather the industry group noted that the nine questions were no longer appropriate if asked of every firm in the industry. After much deliberation, the eventual list had approximately five-hundred questions.

So many questions, of course, implied a level of detail that created problems of confidentiality. A "Big 8" accounting firm was hired to supervise data collection and ensure a "blind transfer" of information to the contractor responsible for the economic analysis. The end result was a one-year delay in the project, perhaps a tripling of EPA's costs, and a huge multiplication of the cost to industry. In the end, neither industry nor the EPA won the data escalation battle.[4]

Indeed, as another example illustrates, a draw in such battles may not be unusual.

The Case of the BCT Criterion

Establishment of a Best Conventional Technology (BCT) criterion for industrial control of water pollutants represented one of the major changes in the 1977 amendments to the Clean

Water Act.[5] The technical debate on the proposals *within* government—critiques and critiques of critiques—illustrates how data and methodology battles often lead to an expensive draw.

The EPA began the BCT standard-setting process by reviewing the "reasonableness" of its existing Best Available Technology (BAT) standards. BAT requirements determined to be reasonable were to be redesignated BCT standards. BAT standards determined to be unreasonable according to the new congressional standard were to be suspended and new, less stringent BCT standards substituted in their place. A general definition of "reasonableness" had been set out in 1977 water pollution control legislation and made clear the congressional intent to relax the requirements on industry. To comply with this definition, the EPA needed to establish a reasonable cost per pound of pollution removed. If one industry experienced costs per pound less than this reasonable level, the EPA could presumably tighten the pollution requirements; if costs were above this benchmark, then rules needed to be relaxed. In this context, the higher the benchmark, the more stringent the pollution control regulations the EPA could justify and still meet the statutory test of reasonableness.

THE INITIAL EPA PROPOSAL

On August 23, 1978, the EPA proposed BCT regulations based on a complicated test to determine whether or not the current BAT conventional guidelines were reasonable for each industrial subcategory. The EPA received comments on its proposed BCT standards from seventy-nine parties. The intense interest of a wide range of industries was not surprising, since the agency had stated its intentions to apply the proposed methodology to a large number of industries. Thus, for example, the pulp and paper industry, an industry that generated a great deal of wastewater, submitted lengthy comments and was a major participant in the rule making even though its BCT standards had not been proposed in the August 23 announcement.

THE COWPS ANALYSIS

The President's Council on Wage and Price Stability (COWPS) also submitted comments on the BCT rule making. COWPS was an independent body within the Executive Office of the President. Its statutory responsibility included the authority to consider the inflationary impact of proposed government regulations and submit comments to the *Federal Register*. The economists in COWPS were highly critical of EPA methodology, arguing that the EPA proposal did not generate cost-effective pollution cleanup.

COWPS put the appropriate benchmark cost between $0.13 to $0.19 per pound of pollution removed. These costs were dramatically lower than EPA estimates, which ranged from $0.40 to $1.39.

THE FINAL RULE: THE $1.15-PER-POUND TEST

On August 29, 1979, the EPA issued final BCT guidelines for selected industries. The final rule ostensibly incorporated COWPS's major methodological recommendations. The EPA explained that the switch from its complicated formula to the COWPS methodology would "result in a more 'economically efficient' solution."

By far the most important characteristic of the final EPA proposal was the level of the BCT benchmark. The figure of $1.15 per pound was actually greater than the EPA's earlier proposal (approximately $0.90) and well above any of the values suggested in the COWPS submission—or in any industry submission, for that matter. Setting a high benchmark for the industrial cost comparison meant that despite an extensive congressionally mandated study that found the BAT requirement too costly for industry, despite an apparent agreement to relax the standards, despite an innovative mandate to implement the relaxation in an economically efficient manner, and despite a further two-year regulatory process in which the EPA developed cost information and obtained detailed comments from almost eighty parties—despite all this, it appeared that very little had changed because of the way the battle over data and methodology had unfolded.

REACTION TO THE EPA DECISION

The agency's final version of the rule on BCT guidelines was issued in the summer of 1979. As observed, the net result of the EPA's deliberations was to leave the industrial effluent standards program largely unchanged. The methodology battle, however, did not stop at that time.

LEGAL CHALLENGES

Soon after the BCT guidelines were published, most of the industries directly affected and many of those indirectly affected sued the EPA.

As a practical matter, court actions tend to be ineffective weapons in the battle over methodology. While it is possible that the courts would overturn the BCT guidelines, it was more likely that they would defer to the EPA on most of the methodological issues. Of course, if the agency had overlooked important data or made an arithmetic error—*procedural* problems exposed in litigation over other rules—the BCT standards would have been (and subsequently were) remanded to the agency. But the overall framework for setting BCT standards—and the methodology used for setting the $1.15 figure—was likely to survive court challenge. The basis for a court's overturning of interpretations of complicated statutes like the Clean Water Act was generally that the agency abused its discretion and had done something legally wrong. While a court might even agree with industry that the EPA *could* have chosen some other interpretation of the BCT mandate, based on a long history of court review of regulatory decisions, a court was not likely to rule against the particular interpretation the EPA settled on provided it was within the agency's legitimate *procedural* discretion. Again, the EPA was held accountable by the courts to process, not to outcome, and the sophisticated EPA decision makers knew it.

In contrast, administrative oversight could deal with the issue of whether the BCT rule *should* be changed (not that it was illegal), and, indeed, such challenges were forthcoming both from industry and the White House. In response, the EPA escalated further the methodology battle and sponsored a costly study to analyze the COWPS methodology and compare it to the EPA's own analysis. The result of this analysis was a demonstration that both the EPA and COWPS methodologies yielded results well within the range of "reasonable outcomes." In other words, the BCT case led to a draw in the methodology contest.

It is not uncommon that a draw is negotiated among the parties trying to forestall time delays and the waste of limited resources. Negotiated settlements of data and methodology have not yet proven themselves, but there is cause for hope. One seemingly successful effort involves the Health Effects Institute described in chapter 10. Its deliberately unrevealing name belies the political efforts necessary to bring together the partners in this enterprise.

The problem was truck and automotive emissions. The cost of data and methodological escalation in this important area of public policy was high and growing rapidly for both vehicle manufacturers and the EPA. The solution was an agreement by all parties to pool research efforts in a single agency and agree to live with the scientific findings. This agreement was not merely an effort to depoliticize science but also to deal explicitly and collaboratively with the politics of science. As such, the success of the Health Effects Institute may be viewed as a precursor of events to come in other battles over truth and science in the area of public policy and competitive interaction.

194 UNDERSTANDING GOVERNMENT

The Danger of Creeping Incrementalism

Just as sophisticated public actors are aware of the threat of methodological capture, they are also aware of the need to overcome "creeping incrementalism." Consider the following case. In 1977 the Weyerhaeuser Company was confronted with several technological options for controlling water pollution at its Longview, Washington, facility.[6] Management was expanding this plant's production capacity and good economics demanded that the firm make reasonable provision for the next round of water pollution controls, then scheduled to be imposed in 1983. Although the EPA had not yet promulgated the 1983 standards, Weyerhaeuser projected that plant effluent after 1980 would be 13,000 pounds per day greater for biological oxygen demand (BOD) and 30,000 pounds per day greater for total suspended solids (TSS) than the anticipated standards, if no new water pollution control processes were installed.

Weyerhaeuser management had three basic options: (1) do nothing until the regulations were made final; (2) invest to meet the anticipated standards or management's "best guess" as to what these standards would be; or (3) choose an investment strategy that hedged the firm's exposure to the risks of regulatory changes in a way management felt politically and economically sensible.

The do-nothing alternative could be very costly because it was cheaper to build compliance capacity during expansion rather than add it on later.

For a number of reasons, the second option was also unattractive. With the effluent reduction capacity already in place by the time the 1983 standards were promulgated, the apparent ease of meeting the new standards might, in a self-fulfilling way, lead to still more stringent standards, with impacts on other Weyerhaeuser facilities and competitors. This might be the case because, after all, the incremental social cost of the new standards measured by the EPA would actually be lower if Weyerhaeuser committed itself early to the announced control levels. Moreover, if Weyerhaeuser invested in compliance but the EPA subsequently chose to reduce the level of effluent control, then the regulatory agency would have hurt a co-operative firm, rewarded procrastinating firms, and sacrificed low-incremental-cost environmental benefits. This, of course, would be an uncomfortable situtation for the EPA as well as Weyerhaeuser management.

If management opted for a hedging strategy as in the third option, then it would lower its current costs but increase both its own incremental costs and the incremental costs to society that the EPA would observe when analyzing the stringency of its new standards. For example, one pollution control option might provide Longview with a near-term advantage. It removed more TSS than any other option and a significant amount of BOD, although it did not reduce effluent sufficient to meet the anticipated requirements. In a dynamic regulatory setting, the selection of a reasonably effective control technology in advance of the promulgation of standards could be seen as a "good-faith" effort and, if the company were lucky, be all that was required.

While Weyerhaeuser's actions would not be the determining factor in EPA decision making by any means, it was true that a former EPA administrator was a senior vice-president in the firm and the Longview facility was one of the largest paper-making operations in the country. More important, Weyer-haeuser was not the only firm in the paper industry making this kind of decision. It was unlikely that the EPA would or could ignore the cumulative economic and political effects of the actions of this firm and its competitors. Realizing this, Weyer-haeuser management might install a less expensive—and less effective—control technology and wait for a decision from Washington. In this instance, the incremental cost of stringent standards would be high and thus perhaps would discourage the EPA from proposing stringent rules. Thus, if the EPA stayed with the rule anticipated by Weyerhaeuser, higher costs would be incurred—incremental costs, that conceivably at least, might no longer be justified by the incremental benefits.

In other words, by choosing the *path* of sequential compliance decisions, Weyerhaeuser, could help determine both its and society's exposure to regulatory uncertainty in politically and economically significant ways.

This example is not intended to make Weyerhaeuser and other firms in the paper industry necessarily appear as trying to "game" the EPA into pursuing some particular action or another. To the contrary, Weyerhaeuser has an excellent record of environmental responsibility. Still, the example shows how subtle strategic decisions not only influence the exposure of firms to altered patterns of incremental costs but change real incremental costs to society as well. Nor is this example intended to show that the EPA operates only to maximize the difference between incremental costs and benefits in some simplistic public interest concept of EPA decision making. Rather the case shows that Weyerhaeuser's decisions played an important role in shaping the circumstances that the EPA would confront in its subsequent decisions, whatever the EPA's objectives. Whether or not Weyerhaeuser was trying to "game" the system, it had no choice but to be a player: in a world where all decisions yield winners and losers, there was no neutral action.

It would be irresponsible of Weyerhaeuser's management to ignore the significance of this kind of strategic decision to its stockholders since the alternative compliance strategies differed by millions of dollars. It also would be irresponsible of the EPA to ignore the incremental costs created by Weyerhaeuser management's decisions. Most important, it would be irresponsible for the EPA not to be sensitive to its possible "capture" by the pattern of cumulative strategic decisions of firms it regulates.

The Weyerhaeuser example also shows that private-sector strategic adaptation to regulation, by itself, is neither good nor evil. Weyerhaeuser might well pursue a compliance strategy that complemented the objectives of environmental policy makers and help advance the nation's environmental goals. It would still alter the pattern of incremental costs facing society and EPA decision makers.

The Weyerhaeuser case is, of course, replicated thousands

of times throughout the economy. Confronting regulation, managers make decisions, the cumulative effect of which is to alter the real incremental costs to society of policy changes and make important public regulatory decisions vulnerable to the cumulative strategic decisions of the regulated enterprises.

The dangers of creeping incrementalism would appear most difficult to fend off when the path of incremental decision making results from cooperation between business and government. When incremental decisions are created by industry "stonewalling," public authorities have a natural incentive to avoid capitulation, but not so when the actions stem from cooperative behavior.

This suggests that sophisticated public actors will be sensitive to drawing limits on the degree of cooperation they received from industry on regulatory matters. This is not to say that business/government relations need to be hostile, as they have often been in the past, but it is to acknowledge that such relations are inherently adversarial, whether or not they are procedurally adversarial. No sophisticated public actor loses sight of this adversarial relationship; indeed, he or she should be alerted to the possible need to look more closely at a regulatory issue when adversarial positions are *not* being taken. While there are many cases in which public and industrial interests do coincide, it is nonetheless appropriate for a sophisticated regulator to question all such circumstances in which this seems to occur.

Chapter 12

Meeting the

Policy Challenge

Throughout the preceding chapters we have stressed that all companies and government agencies share a strategic interest in understanding competition when government matters. We have also seen that the unintended effects of such public intervention often have long-term implications for the U.S. economy. We have already discussed how private managers might cope with these realities. It is now appropriate to ask just what the response of the nation's policy makers and managers ought to be.

There are two extreme possible responses. The first is to ignore the whole problem. The nation has gotten along quite well without dealing explicitly with the competitive consequences of public action in the past, so why start now? The other extreme is to respond aggressively to our new understanding on the grounds that new information is a potentially valuable tool for advancing public purposes. There are persuasive arguments for both approaches.

The Do-Nothing Strategy

If we have gotten by in the past with a "do-nothing" strategy, we can get by in the future—or so one argument would go. Moreover, if the dynamic interactions of business and government are as complex as they now appear, further research will likely show them more complicated still. On the grounds that a little knowledge can be a dangerous thing, it may be wise to avoid the temptation to adapt policy to our still-limited understanding. Let's simply recognize that a fundamental virtue of a market economy is that we do not need to know precisely how it works to take advantage of the fact that it *does* work.

And, of course, the Iron Law of Public Policy itself tells us that whatever we do to adapt policy to our understanding of competitive realities will itself create winners and losers. This will, in turn, trigger both political and economic responses that may necessitate further intervention. Rather than initiate an endless cycle of intervention, it may be better to "let sleeping dogs lie."

The Aggressive Management Strategy

But there is an alternative perspective. According to this view, new knowledge is a valuable asset that should be used to advance public interests. To resist the temptation to use new information aggressively not only smacks of anti-intellectualism but may represent the too-hasty abandonment of a new and potentially valuable policy tool. It may be unwise to preclude the use of new sources of economic control just because they are unfamiliar or subject to misuse. By definition, any new economic policy instrument will be unfamiliar. Moreover, any new instrument with the capacity to do good has the capacity to do harm. As the Consumer Product Safety Commission long ago recognized, the only effective way to make matches completely safe for consumers is to manufacture them so that they cannot light. Similarly, policy instruments with the least capacity for harm are often the ones with the least capacity for good. The potential misuse of economic knowledge, therefore, is not necessarily an argument against aggressive government action but merely an argument in favor of the careful exercise of all government economic power.

Advocates of the aggressive management approach would also observe that this nation's competitors have a growing understanding of the nature of the interaction between public and private economic decision makers. Other governments and multinational enterprises know they can often cooperate to exploit a hands-off U.S. strategy. A do-nothing policy may have served us well in the past when the United States was the clearly dominant international business force, but a more aggressive approach may be needed in the future.

And still another argument for aggressive management of the business/government relationship is that its conscious and systematic management is essential in a political system where meddlers and tinkers always exist and have considerable political strength. Left to their own devices and unconstrained by conscious policy design, these inveterate tinkerers can do substantial harm to economic policy. The nation's Rube Goldberg tax system, for example, is arguably the accumulation of a series of incentives, exemptions, and the like that, when viewed one at a time, have political and economic appeal but, when viewed in the aggregate, hardly represent a strategically coherent tax policy. Advocates of conscious and explicit management of the business/government relationship would caution us that the elusive pursuit of a do-nothing policy runs the risk of turning other aspects of economic policy into the equivalent of the current IRS tax code.

How to Choose

The choice between these approaches ultimately rests on the answers to two questions: What works in practice? And what works in theory? The reason for the first question is obvious—or ought to be. Public policy cannot be usefully viewed simply in the abstract. Policies succeed or fail only when implemented. Policy making cannot be divorced from policy management. The second question is less obvious. Why must a good policy meet the test of good theory as well as good practice? Because no economic policy is static. Today's policy is one more step in a sequence of administrative and policy moves. Because subsequent policy moves are always made under circumstances of less than complete information, theory—even for the most pragmatic of us—necessarily plays an important role in shaping future decisions. It matters, therefore, that policy meet the test of both practical effectiveness and consistency with good theory.

What Works in Practice?

The do-nothing strategy seems to work well in practice. Our economy has prospered without an acknowledged policy of public management of microeconomic affairs. Even during economic recessions, the U.S. economy seems to outperform that of many other industrialized nations which aggressively manage business/government affairs.

But this policy success may be only surface deep. This is not to imply that U.S. economic performance is only superficially successful. To the contrary, its success is real and impressive. What may be surface deep is the notion of a do-nothing policy. Literally the first act of the Congress of the United States was a tariff act affecting the shipment of goods into the United States—the first of a series of policy interventions into business affairs with profound implications for the U.S. economy.[1]

One reason the "do nothing" policy is attractive to some people is that more aggressive policies are often formulated under crisis conditions. Under such conditions, legitimate and compassionate concerns for displaced workers and distressed communities often take policies in directions that might not be

pursued in the absence of crisis or in the presence of a governmental capacity to respond to the human pains of economic
distress. Similarly, calls for intervention rarely occur in noncri-
sis circumstances. Thus, while it is common to come to the aid
of a declining industrial sector, it is less common to marshal
public resources to advance the competitive interests of an otherwise thriving sector. So long as government involvement in
business affairs is considered a response to economic pathology
and not to economic good health, the nation necessarily confronts a limited and possibly a distorted set of policy options.
A do-nothing policy may look attractive only because the alternatives are so narrowly defined at present.

The do-nothing strategy frequently appeals to many practical
individuals because government—its good intentions notwithstanding—is often less capable of handling economic distress
than some of us would like. In medicine, when disease preven-
tion has failed, curative action is sometimes avoided on the
grounds that the cure can be worse than the disease. For government to intervene when an industry is in crisis, having failed
to prevent the crisis from occurring, may be similarly counterproductive. In such circumstances, to do nothing may be the
preferred strategy only because potentially effective actions
were ignored or what could be done was done, but turned out
to be inadequate.

There are additional reasons to conclude that the do-nothing
strategy may not be quite so attractive in practice as it may first
appear. The policy's economic merits notwithstanding, it has
clear political handicaps in a world in which dramatic and visible intervention is less than fully resistible. An analogy lies in
the area of health care. In the political arena a "cure for cancer"
has far greater appeal than a program to prevent it. Similarly,
a cure for some rare disease is also more appealing than a program to prevent lower back pain or cure the common cold,
despite the millions of sufferers and the substantial economic
and social cost of diseases "that never killed anybody." Aggressive intervention, in other words, may be a political necessity,
even if more temperate policies might be appropriate.

And finally, critics of the do-nothing policy can argue that the nation's economic success—which advocates of a do-nothing policy use as their basic argument for nonintervention in business affairs—is merely evidence that the policy works well, not that it works best.

If the do-nothing strategy has its weaknesses, the same can be said of the aggressive management alternative. The notion of "fine-tuning" the macroeconomy for sustained economic growth and stability was once popular among economists. Such a view is no longer in vogue precisely because claims of our ability to manage economic affairs aggressively had been overstated. For every successful intervention critics can now cite one or more failures. While macro- and microeconomic affairs are quite different, it is by no means obvious that aggressive microeconomic management fares any better than its macro counterpart once in place. Many of the nation's departures from the do-nothing strategy have not proven all that successful.

Advocates of aggressive management of business/government affairs often point to the track records of such management in other countries. Increasingly, however, analysts are coming to appreciate that much of the optimism surrounding assessments of policy in other countries has not held up under closer scrutiny or the test of time. Indeed, many advocates of aggressive economic management today find themselves in political and intellectual retreat.

What Works in Theory?

If neither strategy seems to dominate in practice, does either dominate in theory?

It is relatively easy to dismiss the do-nothing strategy on theoretical grounds: because there are always winners and losers, and because all government actions—and inactions—have long-term implications for the shape of the U.S. economy, there is no "do-nothing" policy.

But that is not to say that there is no merit to maintaining the fiction of such a policy. Such a fiction has the practical merit of compelling advocates of intervention to justify more adequately their individual cases. This justification is undoubtedly healthy in a political setting where the temptation to "do something" always appears to dominate that of doing nothing. After all, what manager, public or private, can champion the aggressive pursuit of inaction—despite the frequent merits of such an approach?

While such a burden has considerable appeal, it is not without risk, however, for it encourages ad hoc responses to economic problems. It also encourages well-informed special interests of all persuasions to "play the game" in the arcane details of government rules and procedures, obscure from broader public accountability. As we have seen throughout this book, the opportunities for such intervention and manipulation in pursuit of private interests are substantial. The political and economic risks associated with a mythical do-nothing strategy are real in both theory and practice.

The aggressive management approach is not very attractive from a theoretical perspective either because it suffers from at least three deficiencies.

First, it is presumptuous. The information requirements and institutional discipline necessary are both enormous. Second, even if these obstacles can be overcome, the very argument that makes aggressive management attractive also suggests its ultimate failure: the dynamics of competition are highly complex; public policies shape these dynamics in important ways, triggering strategic responses in both private and public institutions. The very complexity and sophistication of these processes may preclude their effective management.

Third, the ability of all actors to position themselves strategically for whatever action government might take may well preclude successful public intervention. Stated differently, our improved *public* understanding of competition when government matters is matched by an improved *private* understanding of these same forces. This private understanding may increase the ability of those so inclined to undo or distort the actions of government at the same time that better public knowledge would seemingly improve the government's ability to intervene in economic affairs.

Politics Without Apology

Ultimately, the basic criticisms of both the do-nothing and aggressive management strategies come down to legitimate questions of politics. It is unavoidable that decisions of government are important determinants of microeconomic affairs. It is unavoidable that these microeconomic impacts will determine who profits throughout society. These are not issues that can or should be avoided: they are at the heart of what it means to understand competition when government matters. Just as we find no need to apologize for the law of gravity, we have no need to apologize for the political and economic consequences of the Iron Law of Public Policy. Rather, our challenge is to construct economic and political institutions that deal with this reality forthrightly and exploit the political and economic forces unleashed for the broader benefit of society.

This is no small challenge in a world in which the science of politics has been too long separated from the science of economics. (Perhaps it is worth recalling that the first students of economics referred to their new endeavor as "political economy.") It is also no small challenge in a world in which the practice of both political science and economics is often separated from the theory. (Perhaps it is also worth noting that early political economists were known as much for their practical relevance as they were for their intellectual rigor.)

Guidelines for Action

If it is inappropriate to advocate a do-nothing strategy—if only because it is not possible—and it is inappropriate to advocate a program of aggressive management of microeconomic policy —because of our inherently limited capacity to carry it out— what should policy makers and policy managers do to make use of the improvements in our understanding of competition when government matters? Eight guidelines for action emerge from what we now know about the nature of business/government interaction.

1. BEFORE REGULATING BUSINESS, UNDERSTAND THE PROCESS OF REGULATION

It may seem a bit unnecessary to suggest to public managers and policy makers that they must come to understand a process that they live every day, but merely living a process is not the same thing as understanding it. To understand the process of business/government relationships well enough to formulate sophisticated and effective public policies, it is necessary to pay attention to political legitimacy, be aware of the "issue/attention" cycle, and have the capacity to marshall the information on which the policy process depends.

Pay Attention to Political Legitimacy. Regulatory authority is described in statute but granted by the general public. Public mandates and statutory authority do not always coincide. Sometimes statutes convey more legal authority than the public has truly granted. This phenomenon is familiar to police chiefs who find themselves legally responsible for enforcing statutory requirements with no political support—for example, enforcement of Sunday closing laws in some jurisdictions or jaywalking laws in a university community.

Just as Prohibition was unenforceable in the 1920s, regulatory restrictions are often unenforceable today and for the same reason: legislation is typically passed during a period of euphoric public support for some particular regulatory intervention. The letter of the law often fails to survive later political scrutiny, but not necessarily with enough objection to trigger a legislative reversal.

In the 1970 Clean Air Act, for example, many environmentalists thought they had won a major victory by getting language so tough that the failure of the U.S. auto industry to invent new pollution control technology would result in a $10,000 fine per car. This was, of course, false regulatory stringency because no serious observer felt the penalty credible. Indeed, many people argued that a $100 fine would have been more effective just because such a fine was, in fact, thinkable.

Public officials responsible for the emissions control regulatory process had to take the political legitimacy of this unreasonable penalty into account. Thus a sophisticated administrator could not ignore the rule—after all, it was the law—but would not impose regulations with the hope of using this penalty as an enforcement device. Rather, a sophisticated policy maker would recognize that the true authority conveyed by this penalty provision was not the penalty itself but the necessity of the regulated parties to come to some kind of subsequent political accommodation to the nation's environmental goals sufficient to justify a congressional revision of the rule. The real force of this stiff penalty provision was not in its literal application but in its political interpretation.

Sometimes political authority exceeds legal authority. In the early 1970s the political pressure for quick governmental action on pollution control matters ran up against the realities of slow legislative deliberations. To cope with a political need to act, but lacking explicit statutory authority to do so, the Nixon Administration, first through the Corps of Engineers and later the Environmental Protection Agency, resurrected the 1899 Refuse Act. This law had been on the books and ignored for over seventy years with little consequence, due to lack of political mandate. The law contained a provision authorizing the Corps of Engineers to issue permits for the discharge of material in the nation's navigable waterways. The law was initially designed to protect navigation interests and was by no means passed in prescient anticipation of the environmental movement. With creative interpretation of both the concept of navigability and refuse, the corps was able to invoke this law as justification for a pollution control program based on effluent permits. What made invocation of the provisions of this statute acceptable was not legal authority but a political mandate to address pollution problems. Indeed, the legal authority did not survive subsequent court scrutiny, but the act's political legitimacy did survive as a program of industrial permits eventually became the mainstay of the nation's effort to control industrial discharges into our waters.

Once again, the conclusion is that the capacity for public authorities to regulate business stems from public support and not merely statutory authority. Sophisticated public policies reflect this reality.

Recognize the Importance of the Issue/Attention Cycle. Anthony Downs has described the dynamics of what he calls the "issue-attention cycle."[2] According to Downs, public interest in regulatory policies follows a clearly definable five-stage sequence. In the "preproblem stage" an undesirable social condition exists but has not yet captured public attention. This describes the pre-1970 view of the environmental problem. In an April 1965 Gallup survey, for example, when asked to identify the three most pressing national problems from a list of ten, respondents gave reducing water and air pollution ninth priority, above only "beautifying America." By April 1970 reducing pollution was second on the list only to reducing crime.[3]

While on objective grounds the environment had not taken a sudden turn for the worse during this five-year period, the issue had entered Downs's second stage of "alarmed discovery and euphoric enthusiasm." It was during this stage that much of today's environmental and safety legislation was passed.

Downs, writing in 1972, predicted that this second stage

would be followed by stage three: "realizing the cost of significant progress." This growing realization of costs and the associated trade-offs among society's other problems and interests would yield to a "gradual decline of intense public interest" in stage four, followed by a fifth "post-problem stage" in which the issue had "lost its position at the center of public attention."

There is both casual and substantive evidence to suggest that Downs's predictions with regard to environmental policies were accurate. For example, between 1970 and 1980 the percentage of individuals surveyed who placed the reduction of pollution among the nation's three most pressing problems dropped from 53 percent to 24 percent—only 7 percentage points above its level in 1965.[4] But the utility of the Downs's model is not restricted to its predictive power; rather it lies in the implication that what public policy ought to be at any given moment differs depending on the stage of evolution in the issue/attention cycle. Thus, prior to public awareness in the "preproblem" stage, information-based strategies might be most appropriate in preparation for a subsequent public focus of attention. Once public attention is focused by the "alarmed discovery" of a pressing problem, there is likely to be pressure for legislative action. At this stage it might be best for public officials to marshal as much managerial discretion, political support, and legislative backing as possible. While the "optimal" public policy may be unknown at this time, sufficient discretion must be created to pursue whatever that policy might prove to be. Over time, subsequent legislative reforms are likely to be more constraining, not less, as the public realizes the "cost of significant progress." A sense of strategic possibilities, therefore, not optimal policy, is appropriate at the early stages of the issue/attention cycle. For example, since legislation creating a new program is likely to occur during the period of public euphoria, it may make sense to seek the strongest possible goals and widest possible jurisdictional responsibility at that time. There may well be less need politically to deal with subtleties like economic efficiency or regulatory oversight under such circumstances.

As experience with the new policy grows, public interest—but not special interest—wanes. This creates still different demands on public policy. Implementation takes on more importance than legislation, and administrative efficiency takes on a high priority. Moreover, efforts to avoid capture by special interests is essential at this phase of policy evolution.

And finally, awareness of the interest/attention cycle yields the realization that substantive attainment of regulatory goals is most likely to occur during the "post-problem stage." At that time it is neither esoteric legislative goals nor strong public opinion that can move a regulatory program along, but rather organizational capacity and institutional momentum.

The issue/attention cycle makes clear that regulation and hence the business/government relationship must be viewed as a dynamic and evolutionary institutional process. It also reveals that snapshots of the process at any given point in its evolution may reveal "inefficiency" according to static criteria of optimal public policy. Thus, at the initial stage, interventions will be seen as simplistic and myopic, oriented toward unrealistic and costly goals. In later stages of evolution, public authorities will be cast as bureaucratic and inflexible, responding to yesterday's problems rather than today's.

Public actors who wish to respond in a sophisticated strategic manner to the challenge of managing business/government relationships effectively have to come to grips with this conflicting reality: on the one hand, the practicalities of strategic institutional management require actions that on their surface appear inefficient; on the other hand, the inevitable criticisms of these actions will, in themselves, affect managerial discretion, resource levels, and political authority. No public official can expect to manage this tension effectively without a sophisticated understanding of the dynamics of the issue/attention cycle.

Treat Information as Power. Private sector actors who are sophisticated in the ways of business/government affairs know the value of information to the political process. Indeed, while business lobbyists have a public image as checkbook-wielding lawyers with good friends in high places, the reality is that most lobbying activity involves the generation and distribution of information. The reason for this is simply that information is power in the political process. A congressional representative who is given a copy of a study showing how some particular piece of legislation influences his or her district is likely to pay attention to it. Similarly, it is virtually impossible to raise an issue in the political arena without that issue becoming relevant to the political outcome. The importance of information and the related importance of credibility on the part of data providers create a natural incentive for individuals to provide accurate and detailed information.

While information gained through the political process is unlikely to be knowingly inaccurate and certain to be voluminous, it may well be selective: there is no reason or expectation that a private source will provide data contrary to its own interest. Accordingly, public policy is often better informed by data *not* provided than by information readily supplied. When a union lobbyist decries the loss of high-paying jobs due to some public action, it is not unlikely that the employment impact on low-paying jobs is positive; otherwise the union analyst would have felt no need for the modifier.

Because data are so critical both to sound policy making and the working of the business/government process, a sophisticated public manager has to develop both political skills to acquire and verify data and analytical skills for interpreting information provided in a political environment.

2. BEFORE IMPOSING REGULATORY RESTRICTIONS, UNDERSTAND THE REAL COST OF REGULATION

As we have seen throughout this book, the "real costs" of regulation go far beyond the consequences of regulation for the cost of doing business. Rather they include the impacts on domestic and international competition, the impacts on capacity decisions, and the consequences for long-term industrial strategies. In many industries that compete on bases other than cost, such as service, variety, or product reliability, an undue focus on costs can miss much that is important to competitive impact. Similarly, whatever value benefit/cost analysis might have as a basis for regulatory decision making, it is inherently incomplete. In a world in which the Iron Law dictates that there will be winners and losers as a consequence of all regulatory interventions, it is necessary to understand the pattern of these gains and losses. This requires explicit analysis of the incidence of costs and benefits of public action, not merely estimation and comparison of their aggregate levels.

Pay Attention to Cost Structure. As discussed in chapter 4, an industry's cost structure determines the incremental or marginal competitive circumstances in which firms find themselves. Cost structure is an important determinant of the time pattern of cash flow, the risk of exposure to cyclical downturns, and the ability of competitors to meet short-term competitive pricing pressures. In practice, attention to cost-structure issues poses one of the greatest opportunities for policy makers to help shape competitive institutions in a productive manner.

Perhaps the classic cost-structure policy discussed in the popular press is the value-added tax employed by many nations competing with U.S. industry. The portion of this tax that would otherwise be applied to goods produced for export is rebated to the producer. Critics in the United States often argue that this practice constitutes a subsidy. Others argue that little subsidy is involved since the forgone revenue must be made up by increases in other taxes. Whether a subsidy is or is not involved, there is little doubt that this practice effectively lowers the incremental cost of production for export and thereby effects international competitiveness.

Cost structure may be ripe for policy attention, but it is not a painless avenue to pursue. Given the fact that cost-structure changes, like all changes in competitive markets, create their own pattern of winners and losers, and the fact that they are relatively subtle, there is a real danger that such policies will be used as disguised forms of subsidy. The danger does not lie in subsidy per se: after all, subsidies can represent good public policy. The danger is in the creation of potential hidden subsidies that serve individual interests to the detriment of broader public interests. Cost-structure–related policies may be, in other words, among the most potent instruments of policy and among the most easily abused for political purposes.

Pay Attention to Competitive Strategy. The Iron Law of Public Policy tells us that all public interventions in the marketplace create winners and losers. For industries producing relatively homogeneous products like steel, gasoline, or lumber, the winners and losers result largely from differing production costs in individual enterprises. As we saw in chapter 6, for industries that produce more highly differentiated products like automobiles, specialty chemicals, or electronics, the source of gains and losses due to public action often lies in differing competitive strategies.

In paying attention to competitive business strategy, it is useful to ask if there is a dominant industry strategy. Business strategies apply to individual firms, not to industries, but often the economic circumstances confronting individual firms are so similar that they adopt similar strategies. For example, many electric utilities have similar strategies due to the similarity of regulatory practices in different states. The major U.S. automakers have strategies that differ one from another but that look more homogeneous when compared to, say, European producers.

When a dominant strategy is employed, it may make sense to adapt public policy to this reality. Just as it is easier to swim with the tide instead of against it, it may be easier to achieve policy objectives when regulatory requirements complement business strategies rather than frustrate them. Thus U.S. automakers typically compete with relatively broad product lines, making it attractive to impose fuel economy standards on a corporate average basis to complement fleet diversity. Were they narrow product line manufacturers like many European firms, a horsepower-based regulation might be preferable because it would not discriminate against such manufacturers.

While a particular strategy may appear dominant in a given industrial setting, there are likely to exist firms pursuing quite different strategies. The adaptation of regulation to conform to the interests of the dominant business strategy can undermine these contrary strategies. Thus Saab and its single-product automobile line competes quite effectively with General Motors and its broad product line. The same corporate averaging policy for fuel economy standards that aids GM can severely hinder Saab.

The point is that policies should not be twisted or otherwise contorted to conform to the dominant strategic interests. Rather the public manager ought to be aware that the costs of imposing a policy are going to differ both in the aggregate and across competitors to the extent a dominant strategy is complemented or frustrated by public policy.

Before adapting public policy to private strategy, it is necessary to ask if environmental circumstances have dictated a shift in the dominant strategy. Because business strategies are long-lived and characterized by institutional inertia, today's strategies often reflect yesterday's circumstances. Sometimes strategies must change and public policies with them. As we saw in chapter 3, a policy of stringent regulatory standards for leaded gasoline had very different implications for a refinery industry with unwanted excess capacity than for one in which substantial excess capacity was an intentional consequence of its strategic objectives.

Deal with Capacity Impacts. Chapter 5 noted that many of regulation's unintended effects occur through its impact on productive capacity. To understand the capacity implications of public action, it is essential to know what public policy implies for the relative competitive position of new and existing facilities. This single competitive relationship has major consequences for the timing, location, scale, and technological configuration of investments in new capacity.

Perhaps the major way public policy affects this key competitive relationship is through differential regulation: rules and compliance requirements for new facilities more stringent than those for existing facilities. These are often triggered by political fear of imposing regulations so stringent that existing competitors are forced to close or curtail operations. The political merits of such "grandfather" regulatory leniency for existing facilities notwithstanding, an assessment of economic impacts that ignores the strategic consequences of such a bias against new facilities is likely to miss much of what is economically important.

Ask Who Profits. Because so many of the political and economic consequences of public policy stem from the creation of winners and losers, policy makers ought to devote analytical resources to determining who these winners and losers are and why the pattern of gains and losses occurs. Often analysts are uncomfortable addressing these questions because they appear more "political" than "analytical," yet to study who wins and who loses is not the same as taking a normative position regarding the wisdom or fairness of these gains and losses.

There are two practical reasons why explicit analysis of winners and losers is important to sound policy making. First, if much of the political debate is going to surround these competitive issues, information on the nature, extent, and incidence of these impacts is worthwhile having. Second, our intuitive estimates as to who wins and loses with policy intervention is often incorrect due to the complex nature of the unintended impacts of policy.

3. NECESSARY GOVERNMENT INTERVENTION IN THE ECONOMY SHOULD INTRUDE AS LITTLE AS POSSIBLE

The less intrusive government can be, the lower the cost of doing business is likely to be. This has obvious merit in itself but may be less important than the ultimate justification for a minimal intrusion policy: to ensure a robust economy, it is necessary to preserve the strategic options open to corporate managers. Every imposition of an additional social objective on private-sector management—no matter how laudable—complicates the task of management. Public policy may well have to impose significant constraints on business—after all, the nation's concern for the environment, public health, consumer safety, equal opportunity, and the like are all understandable public goals. The challenge is to avoid overconstraining the economic system. For example, it is one thing to impose environmental standards on industry but quite another to prescribe how these standards will be met. Each constraint takes away one degree of freedom from management, but only the imposition of the social objective itself advances the public interest.

This suggests less "command and control" regulation and greater reliance on liability laws, changes in property rights, and financial incentives to advance social goals while keeping strategic discretion in the private sector. The point to be emphasized here is not merely that a policy of least intrusion is attractive ideologically—indeed, some may not find it so—but that basic tenets of decision theory tell us that no economic system can operate effectively without sufficient managerial freedom to achieve the multiplicity of objectives we ask our economic and political institutions to achieve. This is why management strategists tend to be enthusiastic about business strategies that emphasize company focus: by limiting one's objectives, management buys degrees of freedom that it can apply to the narrower and better-defined corporate purposes. The concept applies to government policy as well.

It is also worth stressing that the maintenance of strategic discretion over economic policy in the private sector is *not* necessarily an abdication of public responsibility. To the contrary, the decentralization of economic discretion is consistent with a strategic conception of economic policy in a democratic society, especially when one of the fundamental differences between strategy formulation in the public and private sectors is appreciated.

As just observed, good business strategy typically means

focus: conscious delimitation of a corporation's goals in explicit recognition of the fact that no organization can do all things well. For government policy, good strategy may also require a delimitation of objectives, but such restriction is less likely to mean attention to "focus" in the sense the term is used by corporate strategists than attention to "portfolio" as the concept is used by students of finance. That is, good public policy will not necessarily limit the focus of national efforts but rather recognize that such focus can be risky from a social perspective. Instead, public policy might encourage a mix of private sector strategic responses to economic opportunities. Such an approach has the merit of achieving the benefits of focus in individual firms and the benefits of portfolio in the aggregation of these individual corporate actions. The delegation of strategic decision-making authority to private firms is essential to this conceptualization of sound policy and argues for a program of minimal government intrusion into economic affairs. Such delegation is not intended to leave public policy making to private firms but rather to advance the strategy of the public sector.

4. INSIST THAT SOCIALLY DESIRABLE TRADE-OFFS BE MADE BETWEEN NONECONOMIC AND ECONOMIC GOALS

One of the clear policy dangers created by an improved understanding of competition when government matters is that competitive considerations will intrude excessively into decision processes designed primarily to achieve other worthwhile social objectives. Thus, while it is important that competitive impacts be considered in environmental policy analysis, the primary goal of such policies is ecological and not economic.

This argues rather strongly for a "back to basics" approach to regulatory policy: get the regulatory policy right and the competitive consequences are more likely to be acceptable— even if distasteful to the inevitable losers. At present, economic analysis, let alone strategic industrial analysis, plays too small a role in regulatory affairs. It is also important to note that if the broader trade-offs are correctly made in the aggregate between economic and noneconomic goals, it is much easier to "let the chips fall where they may" when it comes to competitive impacts.

The reason for this is twofold. First, when the economic and noneconomic trade-offs are properly made, the political case for intervention to advance a special economic interest is more difficult to make because such a response would necessitate a sacrifice of legitimate public value. Good policy, in other words, helps insulate the policy process from undue private influence. And second, a proper balancing of economic and noneconomic factors adds political legitimacy not only to the policy itself but to actions designed to remedy the side effects of policy as well. Stated differently, overall competitive business interest in a policy of least intrusion and an adequate policy response to legitimate sources of injury such a policy may entail might ultimately be best served by getting regulatory policy right in the first place. It is a somewhat ironic recommendation in a book devoted to identifying the various indirect competitive consequences of government intervention that policy makers should devote *greater* attention to aggregate benefits and costs of regulatory intervention and less attention to the very microeconomic consequences of policy that have received all our attention.

5. KEEP IT SIMPLE

Another danger from an improved understanding of competition when government matters is the risk of infatuation with the notion of consciously intervening in business affairs to exploit this new knowledge. Such a temptation is to be avoided. The EPA, for example, seeing the competitive implications of environmental controls for the steel industry, once advocated that control requirements be made contingent on industry commitments to certain patterns of reinvestment. Having correctly recognized that environmental policy does influence reinvestment patterns and that the consequences of such impacts are legitimate inputs to public policy decisions, the subsequent decision to use environmental policies to advance nonenvironmental goals was at best risky and at worst a misuse of this improved economic understanding. The EPA was not created to be an agent of economic policy; nor is it accountable to the public or the Congress for its performance as an agent thereof. Moreover, for the EPA to impose on itself the attainment of economic as well as environmental objectives runs the risk of overconstraining the machinery of government such that neither set of objectives is achieved.

Throughout this volume we have seen the complex and indirect consequences of government action for competitive enterprises. To use this evidence to support policies designed to manage cleverly these heretofore unintended consequences would be to misread the basic lesson from these examples: competitive forces are still poorly understood. Awareness of the complexity of such institutional forces is not an invitation to greater micromanagement of the economy but a caution against overzealousness in that micromanagement in which we now engage. Rather than try to be clever, we ought to try instead to get the basics of regulatory intervention correct and avoid the temptation for excessive intervention.

6. THINK POSITIVELY AND USE GOVERNMENT TO AUGMENT COMPETITIVE ADVANTAGES

Typically, government is asked to intervene in the affairs of business to solve problems—environmental pollution, windfall profits, unsafe working conditions, and the like. Given this identification of government action with problems, it is no wonder most of us prefer less governmental involvement in business: less involvement is generally associated with fewer problems. But thinking of government as a response to problems is like thinking about cost reduction as a source of profits: arithmetically, lower costs mean higher profits, but most good managers recognize the limit of cost reduction as the route to profitability. To increase profits significantly, cost reduction helps, but revenue generation is often much more effective.

Similarly, government policies that help solve problems are useful, but they are inherently limited in both scope and potential effectiveness. Government policies that actively advance economic interests, not merely solve problems, are most likely to generate the greatest net benefit to both society at large and economic interests. This leads to the conclusion that government economic policy should be less preoccupied with reacting to competitive disadvantages and instead try to augment competitive advantages.

As an example, consider the local business group in Boston that was recently organized to help identify and solve the problems facing the Massachusetts economy. The first task, accordingly, was to identify the problems needing solution. Not surprisingly, the problems were rather stubborn and difficult to remedy in a cost-effective or politically acceptable manner—that's why they were problems.

Yet the problem orientation was unnecessarily limited and defeatist. Why focus on problems? Massachusetts in the mid-1980s had one of the lowest unemployment rates and highest growth rates of the industrialized states. While the state's economy undoubtedly had its problems, it also had its strengths. Attention to these strengths might well have identified ways to further enhance the state's already attractive competitive position.

For example, the Commonwealth of Massachusetts has high taxes, which have led to the disparaging nickname of "Taxachusetts." There are all manner of explanations for this fiscal situation, ranging from antiquated fiscal practices to the political preferences of the citizenry. In any event, to remedy this problem would obviously be quite difficult; failure of this group to do so would be neither surprising nor unique.

However, for its high tax bills the state has earned a reputation for having some very attractive communities with high-quality schools and local services. These amenities have been a valuable asset to high-technology companies trying to recruit personnel from other parts of the country. As a practical matter, the Commonwealth of Massachusetts might reduce its tax bur-

den on citizens by sacrificing these amenities, but in doing so
it was unlikely to become a low-tax state. Even if it did become
a low-tax state, it would merely be trading a competitive advantage with which it was long associated for one most frequently associated with competing states. And in doing so it
would have alienated all those individuals who had previously
opted for the amenities when choosing a Massachusetts location. Rather than try to change fundamental fiscal conditions,
the more effective business development strategy was likely to
involve efforts that exploited the state's existing advantage in
local amenities. Ironically, exploitation of such an advantage
might actually involve *higher,* not lower, taxes.

The conclusion is generalizable: there are inherent limits to
the good government can perform by trying to remedy competitive disadvantages and solve problems. There is no limit to the
public value that can be created by augmenting competitive
strengths. Accordingly, it is appropriate to adopt a positive
perspective on government microeconomic policy.

7. TRUST THE PROCESS

Business regulation is a process, not merely a specific policy
outcome. Because of this, regulation cannot work effectively
unless people trust the process and consequently allow it to
work. Trust in process does not come easy, and is often the
biggest obstacle to effective and efficient public policy. The lack
of trust creates redundant procedures in the name of accountability, complexity in the name of due process, and inflexibility
in the name of continuity. The result is often the sacrifice of the
very objectives public action was designed to achieve.

Have Faith in Markets. The first manifestation of trust in the
business/government process is faith in markets. It is perhaps
ironic that regulation designed to constrain markets cannot
work unless there is an underlying belief in the efficiency and
fairness of market transactions. The reason for this is that if
markets are inherently corrupt or antisocial then the appropri-

ate policy response is not to modify them on the edges but to eliminate them. To be confident in one's ability to improve the outcome of market transactions through regulation requires a fundamental faith in those very transactions. Moreover, such transactions are themselves among the most potent forms of regulation. To lack confidence in them is hardly to reinforce one's confidence in political and bureaucratic interventions.

Have Faith in Business Managers. As a corollary to faith in markets, public managers need to have faith in their private-sector counterparts. Often business/government relationships turn sour because of the lack of such faith. While due process and the possibility for corruption are legitimate concerns of public managers, it is counterproductive to presume that private sector managers are any less well intended or any less committed to the public interest than people in the public sector. Their ideological views as to what is in the public interest may differ and they may be less well informed substantively on specific policy issues, but to design programs and procedures on the presumption of malevolence is costly and counterproductive.

Thus, for example, the notion that a stiffer fine for regulatory noncompliance is more effective than a less stringent one ignores the fact that few managers wish to operate enterprises that make judgments regarding regulatory compliance on the basis of economic calculus. If the average citizen made the decision to litter or not to litter the highway on the basis of the probability of being fined two hundred dollars for doing so, our streets would be far dirtier than they are now. We depend on goodwill and social consensus to give us clean highways as much as we do fines or cleanup programs. Similarly, effective regulation does not result from successful efforts to cut off all avenues by which regulation can be circumvented, but by creating policies that are sufficiently reasonable from a technical perspective and sufficiently legitimate from a political perspective that compliance is largely self-fulfilling.

To expect to achieve any major regulatory objective entirely by the exercise of police powers of one form or the other is unrealistic. Good public policy necessitates faith in the business managers such policies are designed to constrain.

Have Faith in Consumers. Often a lack of faith in markets is attributable less to a concern for the perceived malevolence of business than to the alleged ignorance of consumers. In just the same way that a lack of faith in markets or in private sector managers can lead to excessive and counterproductive regulation, so can a lack of faith in consumers.

It is easy to assume that consumers are poorly informed on any given consumption choice they make. Who can expect to know all there is to know about the nutritional value of cereals, the longevity and energy consumption patterns of appliances, or the medical implications of alternative anesthetic procedures? And these are only some of the technically complex decisions consumers must make every day.

Yet consumers do not have to be perfectly informed and technically expert to be well informed. With enough personal experience with doctors and the shared experience of families and friends, an individual can come to judge difficult medical choices. It is not easy to know how much energy appliances use and how long they will last, but *Consumers Reports* and similar publications are readily available at the local library or by subscription. And it may be difficult to know what is good for you to eat and what is not, but it is not obvious that the experts know much better. The point is that consumers may not be perfectly informed but that does not make them poorly informed.

Often consumers are criticized for making seemingly irrational decisions. Why, for example, would someone purchase an energy-inefficient window air conditioner when a more efficient model justified the higher cost on a total life-cycle cost basis? Perhaps the answer lies not in the consumer's ignorance but in his or her intent to run the unit only sparingly or because personal financial conditions dictate a discount rate higher than that employed by the regulatory analyst.

As energy prices declined in the mid-1980s and consumers

turned to less fuel-efficient cars, they were criticized as being shortsighted and ignorant of the risks of escalating energy prices in the future. That is one explanation for such behavior. An equally plausible one is that consumers evaluated the risks and were prepared to take them. Or just as likely, they have chosen to purchase a mix of cars that have lower gasoline mileage ratings on average but that positioned them quite well for an emergency. For example, given the choice between owning two cars that each get 27.5 miles per gallon—the 1985 regulatory standard—or one car that gets 20 mpg and a second that gets 37 for an average (as measured for regulatory purposes) of 26, the rational consumer might choose the lower average. In an emergency, by shifting miles driven from the low- to the high-mileage car, this consumer can conserve far more gas than the consumer with two cars at 27.5 and can have the benefit of a larger car when no crisis exists.

It is almost impossible to capture this kind of sophisticated individual decision making in regulation, but allegedly "ill-informed" consumers do it all the time. A presumption of consumer ignorance can lead to counterproductive regulatory intervention.

Accept Success. Trust in the regulatory process necessitates more than trust in markets or people. It also requires a willingness to live with the results of regulatory intervention—results that are often more successful than they are recognized to be.

An example involves the automobile fuel economy standards referred to earlier. According to critics of regulatory leniency, the move by the auto industry and allegedly wasteful consumers to larger cars in the mid-1980s in the face of declining gasoline prices was a setback in the fight to save energy. The facts suggest otherwise. Between the first oil crisis in 1973 and 1985, the pace of technological improvement in automobile fuel economy was so great that despite higher gasoline prices, the incremental energy cost to drive a mile in a new car had actually *dropped* 22 percent after adjusting for inflation. This is one of the nation's great technological and economic successes in which regulatory actions have played a role. Yet, as the consumer takes advantage of some of this dramatic technological and economic improvement by purchasing roomier and higher-performing vehicles, some individuals are inclined to see regulatory failure.

Sophisticated public managers and policy makers need to trust the process, the people who are part of it, and the outcome.

8. THINK STRATEGICALLY ABOUT THE CONSEQUENCES OF GOVERNMENT ACTION DURING POLICY FORMULATION

At present, our use of economic and strategic information in the policy and regulatory process is quite primitive and typically limited to analyses of costs and perhaps some of the indirect strategic impacts of public actions for business. If we are to think positively about government's role in business affairs, there is a pressing need for more sophisticated analytic and strategic thinking about these processes—not because analysis will dictate decision but because sound analysis is essential to assuring that the political decisions be as well informed as possible.[5]

To achieve a strategic perspective on competition when government matters, certain changes in the way governmental decisions are currently made may be required.

Much of the executive branch of the federal government—where many of the policy decisions affecting business are made—operates as a matrix structure that allows affected agencies to reach decisions by consensus. The success of this consensual process depends on the adequacy with which the factors relevant to complex public decisions are represented. At present, strategic business concerns and the competitive effects of public action are considered inadequately, if at all, unless a crisis exists. Strategic business concerns are often represented in a narrowly self-serving way by individual companies or trade associations. Sectoral interests are represented, if at all, by statisticians, economists, and regulators, who tend to be unfamiliar with the requirements of private sector strategic decision making. And without a crisis, even these voices are often ignored.

In principle, it should be easy to establish federal agencies responsible for advancing the well-being of industrial sectors or to augment the role of those agencies that now exist. The key is to recognize the need to include in those agencies strategists as well as economists. Moreover, these agencies should become part of the matrix of organizations party to policy deliberations. If staffed by high-level career civil servants, these agencies might achieve the degree of professionalism and policy continuity now exhibited by the U.S. Department of State and some of the government's statistical agencies.

To represent the strategic concerns of business in the public interest, regulatory authorities must themselves have explicit and well-articulated strategies. To develop such strategies policy makers and managers must ask what specific administrative competence they really demand of their organizations on behalf of the public. Is it cost-effective regulation, with the attendant danger that economic factors will dominate judgmental ones? Is it good science, such that intervenors will be compelled to argue the technical merits of various positions in the hope that such an orientation will move the political dialogue in their particular direction? Is it protection from known societal risks, in which case an aggressive program of technology-based controls may be in order? Is it a concern for innovation, in which case a more diversified program of regulation, economic incentives, and research might be required? It is not necessary to answer these strategic questions here to recognize the need to address them.

The purpose of strategic representation is not to elevate strategic factors to an unduly high level but merely to ensure their inclusion in political and regulatory processes. To guard against undue attention to these matters, it may be necessary to *subdivide* some existing agencies that now possess strategic capacities. Some federal agencies, for example, both represent and regulate specific industrial sectors—as did the former Atomic Energy Commission. Such agencies need to be divided to ensure that policy reflects—but does not become captive of—strategic business factors.

Finally, a creative *tension* should exist among the agencies charged with regulatory policy, sectoral promotion, and overall economic policy. The goal is not to create a superagency wherein winners and losers will be chosen among industrial sectors but rather a governmental structure in which a proper policy tension is created among various social objectives. Good economic performance is too important a social objective *not* to be represented adequately in governmental affairs. It is by no means the sole purpose for public action, however, and should not be accorded undue preference. The trick is to balance competing objectives and force hard choices on an informed government.

The Positive-Sum Challenge

The Iron Law tells us that all regulatory and policy interventions create winners and losers in the marketplace. This political characteristic is inherent to public action. As such, it is not something to be apologized for but something to be managed. Regulators can respond to this reality by standing behind procedure and trying to maintain the institutional fiction of pursuing a strictly scientific or technical approach to regulatory issues. This approach cannot avoid the political consequences of regulatory intervention but can channel political forces in certain ways, perhaps with positive results. This is a not-uncommon governmental approach to problems and has been used with success in many quasi-judicial settings, for example. Such an approach is especially appropriate for dealing with what analysts call "zero-sum games": situations in which one person's gain is necessarily another person's loss. This approach should not be dismissed casually as an appropriate means for conducting regulatory affairs.

But the management of business/government relationships, if it is to achieve its broad social purposes, should not be viewed generally as a zero-sum game where every public gain is at the expense of a completely offsetting private loss. Business regulation is more appropriately viewed as a "positive-sum game" in which there are winners and losers, but the gains are intended to exceed the losses. Such a view is realistic both economically and politically—or at least it can be. The potential for positive economic gain is apparent: no one would be so naïve as to suggest that today's regulatory mechanisms come so close to perfection that there is no room to lower costs without sacrificing noneconomic social goals. The potential for political gain is also clear: citizens are consumers of goods and services produced both in the marketplace and as a consequence of government action. Special interests may view the business/government relationship as "us versus them," but for the average citizen "us" and "them" are one and the same.

A strategic approach to the management of business/government relations is essential to a positive-sum perspective on policy intervention in the marketplace. An appreciation of the dynamic economic and political implications of regulatory action is an integral part of it. Business cannot deal effectively with government without its own strategic perspective; and government cannot deal effectively with business without a similar strategic perspective. The public's interest in a positive-sum relationship between these two sets of institutions that dominate our economic life is not possible without such a perspective.

Concluding Observation

There is no doubt that the federal government has much to do to accommodate effectively our improved understanding of competition when government matters. It is similarly true that state and local governments face their own challenges in this arena. Yet it is also clear that public action cannot be restricted to public agencies. Managers in the private sector have no less an obligation to see to it that the processes of business and government interaction work. This means increased attention to political processes and strategic regulatory impact analysis as well as an appreciation of the legitimately political character of decisions in this important area. The fiction of separation between the public and private sectors, no matter how convenient, must be abandoned. Rather, the whole notion of the strategic interdependence of the public and private sectors must permeate the entire policy apparatus—not to displace other considerations but to sensitize decision makers in both the public and private sectors to the full range of implications of the actions they take.

If advocates of good government can correctly observe that the business of business is too important to society to be left to the private sector alone, then it likely follows that the business of government is too important to be left to the public sector alone. If our improved understanding of competition tells us nothing else, it tells us that business and government cannot be viewed as essentially independent institutions only occasionally interacting with one another. If we truly understand competition when government matters, we recognize that business *is* the business of government and government *is* the business of business.

Notes

Chapter 1

1. For a discussion of the economic implications of this reality, see James Buchanan et al., eds., *Toward a Theory of a Rent-Seeking Society* (College Station, Texas: Texas A&M University Press, 1980).

2. Clint Oster, under the supervision of John R. Meyer, "Monterey Abalone Farms," in Robert A. Leone, *Government Regulation of Business: Developing the Managerial Perspective,* (Boston: Division of Research, Harvard Business School, 1981), pp. 5–25.

3. Ray Palmer, under the supervision of Robert A. Leone, "Nova Products, Inc." (Boston: Graduate School of Business Administration, Harvard University, 1978), HBS Case Services #9-678-045.

4. William A. Niskanen, chairman, *Report of the Working Group on the Alaska Natural Gas Pipeline,* 18 June 1981; Robert Hershey, Jr., "U.S. Backs Pipeline Waivers," *New York Times* (8 October 1981), p. 11, and "Producers of Alaska Gas Win Victory in House for Pipeline," (10 December, 1981), p. 1.

5. U.S. Department of Energy, *Macroeconomic Consequences of Alternative Natural Gas Pricing Policies,* Appendix to *A Study of Alternatives to the Natural Gas Policy Act of 1978,* (Washington, D.C.: U.S. Dept. of Energy 1981).

6. Ira C. Magaziner and Robert B. Reich, *Minding America's Business: The Decline and Rise of the American Economy* (New York: Vintage Books, 1983).

7. For a related discussion of the limits of the liberal political perspective in examining business/government issues, see Robert A. Leone, "Examining Deregulation," *Harvard Business Review* (July–August 1984): 56.

8. William Jackson, under the supervision of Robert A. Leone, "TRIS and Children's Sleepwear" (Boston: Graduate School of Business Administration, Harvard University, 1977), HBS Case Services #9-678-145.

9. Howard K. Gruenspecht, "Differentiated Regulation: The Case of Auto Emissions Standards," *The American Economic Review* (May 1982): 328–31.

10. *Forbes,* 10 September 1984, p. 41, and José Gomez-Ibanez, Robert A. Leone, and Stephen O'Connell, "Restraining Auto Imports: Does Anyone Win?" *Journal of Policy Analysis and Management,* 2 (1983): 196–219.

11. See Peter Bohn, *Deposit Refund Systems* (Baltimore: Johns Hopkins University Press, 1981) for an analytical elaboration of this point and a discussion of other effects of regulation on consumers and producers.

12. Robert A. Leone and David A. Garvin, "Regulatory Cost Analysis: An Overview," *Environment Impact Assessment Review,* 2 (1981): 39–62.

13. Robert A. Leone, "Competition and the Regulatory Boom," in Paul MacAvoy et al., *Government Regulation of Business: Its Growth, Impact and Future* (Washington, D.C.: Council on Trends and Perspective, Chamber of Commerce of the United States, 1979), pp. 27–42.

14. International Research and Technology Corporation, *The Economic Impact of Potential Regulation of Chlorofluorocarbon-Propelled Aerosols,* report prepared for the Environmental Protection Agency, April 1977.

15. Leone and Garvin, "Regulatory Cost Analysis," pp. 42–44.

16. José A. Gomez-Ibanez, "Recision of the Passive Restraint Standard: Costs

and Benefits" (John F. Kennedy School of Government, Harvard University, 1983), Case #C16-83-562.

17. Robert A. Leone, William J. Abernathy, Stephen P. Bradley, and Jeffrey A. Hunker, *Regulation and Technological Innovation in the Automobile Industry*, report prepared for the Office of Technology Assessment, July 1980.

18. Dale W. Jorgenson, *The Macroeconomic Effects of Natural Gas Price Decontrol*, in "Macroeconomic Consequences of Natural Gas Decontrol," Appendix C to *A Study of Alternatives to the Natural Gas Policy Act of 1978.*

19. Gruenspecht, "Differentiated Regulation."

20. Leone and Garvin, "Regulatory Cost Analysis," pp. 54–57.

21. For a general overview see Robert W. Crandall, *Controlling Industrial Pollution: The Economics and Politics of Clean Air* (Washington, D.C.: The Brookings Institution, 1983).

22. James Q. Wilson, ed., *The Politics of Regulation* (New York: Basic Books, 1980).

23. See, for example, Sharon Oster, "The Strategic Use of Regulatory Investment by Industry Sub-groups," *Economic Inquiry* (October 1982): 604–18.

24. George J. Stigler, "The Theory of Economic Regulation," *The Bell Journal of Economics and Management Science* 2, no. 1 (Spring 1971): 3–21.

25. *Economic Report of the President* (Washington, D.C.: U.S. Government Printing Office, February 1982).

Chapter 2

1. This and subsequent quotes are from Clint Oster, "Monterey Abalone Farms (A)," under the supervision of John R. Meyer, in Robert A. Leone, *Government Regulation of Business: Developing the Managerial Perspective*, (Boston: Graduate School of Business Administration, Harvard University, 1981), HBS Case Services #9-981-001.

2. The author's interview with George Lockwood provided additional information not contained in the Harvard Business School case study, as did the NBC television documentary "If Japan Can, Why Can't We?" telecast 24 June, 1980, 9:30 to 11:00 P.M.

Chapter 3

1. Paul W. MacAvoy, "F.D.A. Regulation—at What Price?" *New York Times*, 21 November 1982, p. F3.

2. Robert W. Crandall, "What Have Auto-Import Quotas Wrought?" *Challenge* (January–February 1985): 41.

3. Robert A. Leone, Richard Startz, and Mark Farber, "The Economic Impact of the Federal Water Pollution Control Act Amendments of 1972 on the Paper and Pulp Industry," National Bureau of Economic Research, Inc., report prepared for the National Commission on Water Quality, 15 June 1975.

4. Murray L. Weidenbaum, "The High Cost of Government Regulation," *Challenge* (November/December 1979): 37.

5. Ray Palmer, under the supervision of Robert A. Leone, "Nova Products, Inc." (Boston: Graduate School of Business Administration, Harvard University, 1978), HBS Case Services #9-678-045.

6. International Research and Technology Corporation, *The Economic Impact of Potential Regulation of Chlorofluorocarbon-Propelled Aerosols,* report prepared for the Environmental Protection Agency, April 1977.

7. Ray Palmer, "Nova Products, Inc."

8. For an explanation of this concept, see W. J. Baumol, *Economic Theory and Operations Analysis* (Englewood Cliffs, N.J.: Prentice-Hall, 1972), p. 568.

9. International Research and Technology Corporation, *The Economic Impact of Potential Regulation of Chlorofluorocarbon-Propelled Aerosols,* section 3, p. 26.

10. Stephen P. Bradley and Robert A. Leone, "Federal Energy Policy and Competitive Strategy in the U.S. Automobile Industry," *Annual Review of Energy* 7 (1982): 61–85.

11. Robert B. Leavitt, under the supervision of Robert A. Leone, "Regulating Lead in Gasoline (Cambridge, Mass.: John F. Kennedy School of Government, Harvard University, 1983), Case #C15-83-560.

12. "Costs and Benefits of Reducing Lead in Gasoline: Final Regulatory Impact Analysis," Economic Analysis Division, Office of Policy Analysis, Office of Policy, Planning and Evaluation. (Washington, D.C.: U.S. Environmental Protection Agency, February 1985).

13. For example, see A. Heidenheimer, ed., *Political Corruption: Readings in Comparative Analysis* (Holt, Rinehart and Winston, 1970), and D. Gould, *Bureaucratic Corruption and Underdevelopment in the Third World: The Case of Zaire,* (New York: Pergamon, 1980).

14. J. Royce Ginn, Anne Hill, and Edward V. Blanchard, Jr., *The Economic Impact of the Federal Water Pollution Control Act Amendments of 1972 on the Metal Finishing Industry,* (National Bureau of Economic Research, 15 June 1975).

15. Bradley and Leone, "Federal Energy Policy," pp. 83–84.

16. C. James Koch, and Robert A. Leone, "The Clean Water Act: Unexpected Impacts on Industry," *Harvard Environmental Law Review,* 3 (1979): 90.

17. John Jackson and Robert A. Leone, "The Political Economy of Federal Regulatory Activity: The Case of Water Pollution Controls," in G. Fromm. ed., *Studies in Public Regulation* (Washington and Cambridge, Mass.: National Bureau of Economic Research and MIT Press, 1981), p. 232.

18. Technology and Management Systems, Inc., *Regulatory Cost of Compliance: Comparison of Estimated and Reported Costs and Assessment of Costing Methodologies,* report prepared for the National Science Foundation, 30 November 1984, p. 40. (See also addendum sheet reference to p. 21 of this report.)

19. Title 33 U.S. Congress Sections 1251–1276 (1976). Section 1311 (B) (2) (A) (amended 1977) discusses the "best available technology" standards that differentiate between individual sources of discharge. Federal Water Pollution Control Act.

20. Title 33 U.S. Congress Sections 1251–1276, Sections 1311(B) and 1314(B) (1976). Federal Water Pollution Control Act in U.S. Code, 1982.

21. Koch and Leone, "The Clean Water Act," p. 101.

22. See Koch and Leone, "The Clean Water Act," pp. 104–5, for further discussion on this point.

23. Jackson and Leone, "The Political Economy of Federal Regulatory Activity: The Case of Water Pollution Controls," pp. 248–64.

24. Robert A. Leone, *Environmental Controls* (Lexington, Mass.: D. C. Heath, 1976) pp. 117–18.

25. J. Ronald Fox, "Chain Saws (A), (B), and (C)" (Boston: Graduate School of Business Administration, Harvard University, 1982), HBS Cases Services #9-382-086/7/8.

Chapter 4

1. Robert W. Crandall, *Controlling Industrial Pollution: The Economics and Politics of Clean Air* (Washington, D.C.: The Brookings Institution, 1983), p. 44.

2. Resource Consulting Group, Inc., *Third Party Financing of Industrial Energy Efficiency Projects,* report prepared for the Alliance to Save Energy, Washington, D.C., 28 May 1982, pp. 2.1–2.12.

3. *Final Report on the Federal Highway Cost Allocation Study,* U.S. Department of Transportation (Washington, D.C.: U.S. Government Printing Office, May 1982.)

4. J. Royce Ginn, Anne Hill, and Edward V. Blanchard, Jr., *The Economic Impact of the Federal Water Pollution Control Act Amendments of 1972 on the Metal Finishing Industry* (Cambridge, Mass.: National Bureau of Economic Research, 15 June 1975.)

5. 1983 General Motors Public Interest Report (Detroit: General Motors Corporation, 2 May 1983) p. 37.

6. Statement of Professor William Nordhaus before the House Subcommittee on Telecommunication, Consumer Protection and Finance, 27 and 30 April 1982 (Washington, D.C.: U.S. Government Printing Office) pp. 119–20.

7. 1985 General Motors Public Interest Report (Detroit: General Motors Corporation, 15 May 1985), pp. 21–26.

Chapter 5

1. Robert W. Crandall, *Controlling Industrial Pollution: The Economics and Politics of Clean Air* (Washington, D.C.: The Brookings Institution, 1983), p. 44.

2. *Statistical Abstract of the United States 1985* (Washington, D.C.: U.S. Bureau of the Census, 1984), p. 712.

3. *Statistical Abstract,* p. 712 and *Economic Report of the President* (Washington, D.C., February 1985), p. 234.

4. Robert A. Leone, ed., *Environmental Controls: The Impact on Industry,* (Lexington, Mass.: D. C. Heath, 1976), Chap. 3.

5. John R. Meyer and Robert A. Leone, "Capacity Strategies for the 80s," *Harvard Business Review* (November-December 1980): 133–40.

6. Howard K. Gruenspecht, "Differentiated Regulation: The Case of Auto Emissions Standards," *American Economic Review* (May 1982): 328–30.

7. Arthur D. Little, Inc., *Economic Impacts of Pulp and Paper Industry Compliance with Environmental Regulations,* prepared for the Environmental Protection Agency (Cambridge, Mass., 1977).

8. See *Statistics of Paper, Paperboard and Woodpulp: 1984* (New York: American Paper Institute, October 1984) pp. 30–33. Statistics on newsprint capacity reveal modest increases from 1972 to 1979, but substantial increases following the second oil supply disruption of 1979.

9. Anthony M. Solomon, *Report to the President: A Comprehensive Program for the Steel Industry,* December 1977.

Chapter 6

1. For a discussion of basic principles of corporate strategy and their relationship to government policy, see William Abernathy, Stephen Bradley, and Rob-

ert A. Leone, *Regulation and Technological Innovation in the Automobile Industry* for the Congressional Office of Technology Assessment (June 1980).

2. Robert A. Leone, *Corporate Average Fuel Economy: A 1985 Perspective,* report prepared by Putnam, Hayes, and Bartlett, Inc., for the Automobile Importers of America, May 1985.

3. Annual Report of the Ford Motor Company (Dearborn, Mich., 1983), p. 3.

4. William Abernathy, Stephen Bradley, and Robert A. Leone, *Regulation and Technological Innovation in the Automobile Industry.*

5. Robert A. Leone and Stephen P. Bradley, "Federal Energy Policy and Competitive Strategy in the U.S. Automobile Industry," *Annual Energy Review* (1982): 61–84.

6. "Detroit Adjusts to Downsizing," *Business Week,* 19 June 1978, p. 26.

7. José A. Gomez-Ibanez, Robert A. Leone, and Stephen A. O'Connell, "Restraining Auto Imports: Does Anyone Win?" *Journal of Policy Analysis and Management* 2, no. 2 (1983): 196–219.

Chapter 7

1. Richard Zeckhauser and Aanund Hylland, "Automobile Insurance" (Cambridge, Mass.: John F. Kennedy School of Government, Harvard University, 1982), Case #C15-80-550.

2. Ibid., p. 70.

3. Langdell Baker, *Institutional Investor,* March 1981; *Wall Street Journal,* 30 April 1981; *U.S. News and World Report,* 9 March 1981.

4. For a more formal discussion of the regulatory process as the equivalent of a game, see Bruce M. Owen, *The Regulation Game: Strategic Use of the Administrative Process,* (Cambridge, Mass.: Ballinger, 1978).

5. Bram Johnson, under the supervision of Robert A. Leone, "ITT Rayonier, Inc." in Robert A. Leone, *Government Regulation of Business: Developing a Managerial Perspective* (Boston: Division of Research, Harvard Business School, 1981) pp. 27–37.

6. Lacy Glenn Thomas, "Revealed Bureaucratic Preference of the Consumer Products Safety Commission," working paper, Columbia University Graduate School of Business, 1983.

7. I recall the details of this example from personal conversations with Anthony Cortese.

8. Robert A. Leone, James Meehan, and David Garvin, *The Coca-Cola Decision and the Refillable Container,* report by Charles River Associates, Cambridge, Mass., 11 April 1980.

Chapter 8

1. The reference to the "bird and bunny people" occurred in a casual conversation and was not made in any kind of a derogatory or judgmental manner but to provide a humorous political contrast to the "conservative Republican suburbanite." For a discussion of the public policy and competitive impacts of soft drink container regulation, see Daniel Rose, "National Beverage Container Deposit Legislation: A Cost-Benefit Analysis," *Journal of Environmental Systems* 12, no. 1 (1982–83): 71–84.

2. Joshua Tripper, under the supervision of Phillip B. Heymann, "Auto Safety (A)" (Cambridge, Mass: John F. Kennedy School of Government, Harvard University, 1982), Case #C14-76-141.

3. Thomas J. Peters and Robert H. Waterman Jr., *In Search of Excellence* (New York: Harper & Row, 1982), chap. 9.

4. For a more detailed discussion of the need to keep politics in the regulatory process, see Robert A. Leone and John Jackson, "Toward More Effective Organization for Public Regulation," in W. Abernathy and D. Ginsburg, eds., *Government, Technology and the Automobile* (New York: McGraw-Hill, 1980).

5. Robert A. Leone, "Block Billing of Natural Gas," report prepared by Putnam, Hayes and Bartlett, Inc., for the Citizens Energy Corporation, Cambridge, Mass., October 1985.

6. For one illustration of this phenomenon in the electric utility industry, see "Florida Power & Light (B)" (Boston: Harvard Business School, 1976), Case #9-676-133.

Chapter 9

1. This chapter is based on material derived from the author's personal interview of John Kaneb and information contained in the following case studies by Tim Greening, under the supervision of Robert A. Leone: "Energy Corporation of Louisiana (A)" in Robert A. Leone, *Government Regulation of Business: Developing a Managerial Perspective* (Boston: Division of Research, Harvard Business School, 1981); "Energy Corporation of Louisiana (B)," (Boston: Graduate School of Business Administration, Harvard University, 1978), HBS Case Services #9-678-055; and "Energy Corporation of Louisiana (C)," (Boston: Graduate School of Business Administration, Harvard University, 1980), HBS Case Services #9-680-047.

Chapter 10

1. *Emergency Preparedness,* report prepared by the National Petroleum Council, 1981.

2. John R. Meyer, Clint V. Oster, Jr., Ivor P. Morgan, Benjamin A. Berman, and Diana L. Strassman, *Airline Deregulation: The Early Experience* (Boston: Auburn House, 1981), pp. 7, 8.

3. Confirmed by telephone conversation with Robert Demallie of Cummins Engine Corporation, 2 December 1985.

4. Confirmed by telephone conversation with Michael Clay of Corning Glass Company, 2 December 1985.

5. J. Ronald Fox, "Chainsaws (A), (B) and (C)" (Boston: Graduate School of Business Administration, Harvard University, 1982), HBS Case Services #9-382-086, #9-382-087, and #9-382-088.

6. Thomas Griffith, "Weyerhaeuser Gets Set for the 21st Century," *Fortune* (April 1977), pp. 75–88.

7. URS Research Company, *The Economic Impacts on the American Paper Industry of Pollution Control Costs,* report prepared for the American Paper Institute (San Mateo, Calif.: URS Company, September 1975).

Chapter 11

1. I recall this conversation vividly because it occurred during an interview in which I was trying to question this individual on an unrelated matter. The conversation kept returning to this frustrating incident.

2. Eugene Bardach and Robert A. Kagan, *Going By the Book: The Problem of Regulatory Unreasonableness* (Philadelphia: Temple University Press, 1982).

3. Comments of Felix Rohatyn before the United States International Trade Commission, Investigation No. TA-201-51, May 1984.

4. I recall this incident from personal experience. It occurred during the preparation of "Report to the Environmental Protection Agency" by Meta Systems, Inc., Cambridge, Mass., 17 March 1981.

5. "Best Conventional Technology," (Cambridge, Mass.: John F. Kennedy School of Government, Harvard University, 1983), Case #C94-83-559.

6. Bram Johnson, under the supervision of Robert A. Leone, "Weyerhaeuser-Longview" (Boston: Harvard Business School, 1977), HBS Case Services #9-678-066.

Chapter 12

1. The first act of Congress was the Tariff Act of 1789, July 4 (1 Stat., L.24), effective August 1, 1789. In Joseph N. Kane, *Famous First Facts* (New York: H. W. Wilson, 1981) p. 632.

2. Anthony Downs, "The Political Economy of Improving Our Environment," *Environmental Decay,* ed. Joe Bain (Boston: Little, Brown, 1973), p. 79.

3. Resources for the Future, *Public Opinion on Environmental Issues,* report prepared for the Council on Environmental Quality (Washington, D.C.: Government Printing Office, 1980), p. 7.

4. *Public Opinion on Environmental Issues,* p. 7.

5. Robert A. Leone and Stephen P. Bradley, "Toward an Effective Industrial Policy," *Harvard Business Review* (November–December 1981): 91–97.

Index